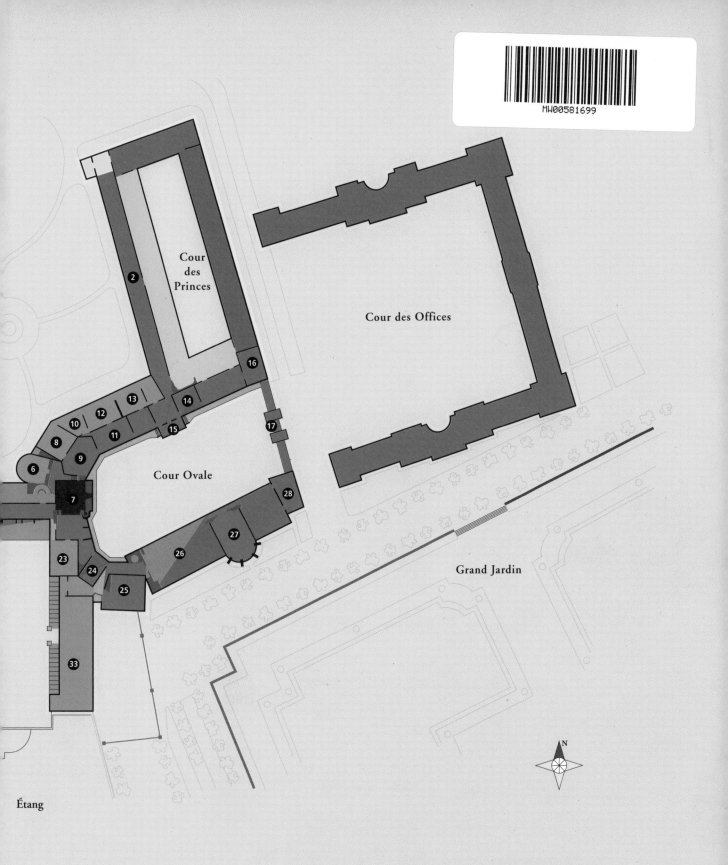

Cour
des
Princes

② 2

Cour des Offices

⑯ 16

⑬ 13   ⑭ 14

⑫ 12

⑩ 10   ⑮ 15   ⑰ 17

⑧ 8   ⑪ 11

⑥ 6   ⑨ 9

⑦ 7

Cour Ovale

㉘ 28

㉗ 27

㉓ 23

㉖ 26

㉔ 24

Grand Jardin

㉕ 25

㉝ 33

Étang

N

15 - Portique de Serlio
16 - Pavillon des Enfants
17 - Porte du Baptistère
18 - Horseshoe-shaped flight of steps
19 - Vestibule
20 - Galerie François Premier
21 - Unnamed Pavilion
22 - Queen-mothers' wing

23 - Salle des Gardes
24 - Bedchamber of the Duchess of
     Étampes, then Escalier du Roi
25 - Pavillon de la Porte Dorée
26 - Salle de Bal
27 - Saint-Saturnin chapel
28 - Pavillon des Dauphins
29 - Pavillon de la Grotte des Pins

30 - Napoleon III's Theatre in
     Louis XV wing
31 - Louis XV wing
32 - Gros Pavillon (in the Pavillon
     des Poêles)
33 - Wing of the Belle Cheminée

FONTAINEBLEAU

FONTAINEBLEAU

Jean-Marie Pérouse de Montclos

Photographs by Georges Fessy

Scala Books

ACKNOWLEDGEMENTS

Jean-Marie Pérouse de Montclos, Georges Fessy and Éditions Scala would like to thank Monsieur Amaury Lefébure, General Curator in charge of the Musée National of the Château of Fontainebleau for his efficient help in the realisation of this book, and Anne Sefrioui for her cooperation.

Éditions Scala would like to thank Hélène Servant, Curator of the Département des Cartes et Plans at the Archives Nationales, and Herveline Pousse from the photographic service at the Réunion des Musées Nationaux.

First published in 1998 by Scala Books
an imprint of Philip Wilson Publishing
143-149 Great Portland Street
London W1N 5FB

Distributed in the USA by
Antique Collectors' Club
Market Street Industrial Park
Wappingers Falls
New York, NY 12590
USA

© 1998 Éditions Scala

Translated from French by Judith Hayward
Edited by Nell Graville
Layout and production: Frédéric Célestin and Thierry Renard
Picture research: Catherine Berthoud

ISBN 1 85759 191 7

Cover: *The horseshoe-shaped flight of steps*

Endpapers: First-floor plan of the château of Fontainebleau,
Thierry Renard, 1998

No book on the château of Fontainebleau has been published since the standard reference work, *Le Château de Fontainebleau* by Félix Herbet in 1937: a scholarly book, without illustrations and not widely available.

The *Guide du musée national du château de Fontainebleau* published in 1991 brought existing information about the collections up to date, and we are greatly indebted to Jean-Pierre Samoyault, the author of the guide and curator of the museum at the time, both for his knowledge of the collections and for their continued development. Study of the architecture of the château and its interior furnishing has come a long way in the last twenty years or so – in particular since the important exhibition devoted to the School of Fontainebleau organised by André Chastel in 1972 – and this is thanks to the work of Sylvie Béguin, Yves Bottineau, Françoise Boudon, Catherine Grodecki, Jean Guillaume and Henri Zerner, which is mainly published in specialist journals, apart from the major study by Zerner which was published in 1996 under the title *L'Art de la Renaissance en France. L'invention du classicisme*. Research into the architecture of the château during the reign of Francis I which has been carried out by Françoise Boudon and Jean Blécon over several years is now nearing completion.

This work, which contains previously unpublished theories regarding a number of points, is aimed at a public that has sometimes been discouraged by the complexity of the château, despite the fact that Fontainebleau can justly be described as the second royal residence – after Versailles – in the whole of France.

CONTENTS

TIME 9

Francis I 10

*Francis I and Fontainebleau • His predecessors: foundation of the castle
and the Couvent des Mathurins • Building work from 1527 to 1535 •
The mason and the architect • Italians in France: Rosso and Primaticcio •
Emperor Charles V's visit • Serlio and Cellini: artists in the king's service.*

From Henri II to Henry IV 34

*Henri II's reign, the Pléiade • The painters active at Fontainebleau
in the second half of the sixteenth century, Nicolò dell'Abate, Caron, Cousin,
the Clouets • De l'Orme in the service of Henri II • The last Valois kings •
Henri IV • the Francinis and the gardens, Matthieu Jacquet and the Belle Cheminée •
The painters Dubreuil, Fréminet, Dubois.*

The School of Fontainebleau 54

*The two schools of Fontainebleau • The Galerie François Premier •
The Galerie d'Ulysse • The Salle de Bal • The three styles of the First School
of Fontainebleau • Galerie de Diane, the story of Clorinda
and the story of Theagenes • The Trinité church •
The School of Fontainebleau and international Mannerism.*

From Louis XIII to Louis XVI.
And From Napoleon I to Napoleon III 94

*Louis XIII and Anne of Austria • Louis XIV • Louis XV
Louis XVI • Napoleon I • From the Restoration to the present day.*

PLACE 129

The Cour Ovale 133

*The Pavillon de la Porte Dorée • The royal apartments •
The Portique de Serlio • The Pavillon des Enfants, the Salle du Guet,
the Pavillon des Dauphins, the Porte du Baptistère,
Saint-Saturnin chapel • The Salle de Bal.*

The Cour du Cheval blanc 165

*The destruction of the Couvent des Mathurins • The building forming the back
of the court • The wings on the court • The horse, the moat, the Jeu de Paume.*

The Cour de la Fontaine, the Gardens, the outlying buildings 194

*The Cour de la Fontaine • The Jardin de Diane
The Cour des Offices, the Cour des Mathurins and the Cour des Princes •
The Jardin des Pins and the Jardin Anglais • The Grand Jardin •
The park, the waterfalls, the canal, and other outlying buildings*

Notes 236
Chronology 239
Bibliography 241
List of Illustrations 242
Index 246

TIME

In the château of Fontainebleau, time and place are intricately interwoven. In order to reconstruct the work carried out during one king's reign, the complete château needs careful examination; to understand the history of a single building or room, several centuries need to be taken into account.

Part One of this book traces the thread of history, revealing the monarchs, the artists they employed and the events they shaped, as they gradually unfold.

Francis I was not the founder of the château, although the structure that can be seen today, built on the ruins of a castle or monastery, was essentially his creation. It was Francis I who assembled the famous artists such as Rosso, Primaticcio, Cellini and Serlio, who are collectively known as the School of Fontainebleau.

Francis I's successors, engaged in doing, undoing and redoing work, were mainly involved in creating interior decorations. These interiors are introduced and described in Part One of this book, where the aim is to bring back to life interiors that have since been broken up, and to "restore" to Fontainebleau elements that are no longer there. As a result, the locations are only of secondary interest, and it should be possible to follow the gist of the argument without being familiar with the general layout of the château, which is introduced in Part Two.

Francis I

Francis I and Fontainebleau • His predecessors: foundation of the castle and the Couvent des Mathurins • Building work from 1527 to 1535 • The mason and the architect • Italians in France: Rosso and Primaticcio • Emperor Charles V's visit • Serlio and Cellini: artists in the king's service

The fate of the château of Fontainebleau was perhaps decided at the Battle of Pavia (1525) when Francis I lost everything "except for honour": the laurels gained by his victory at Marignano, some of his oldest comrades-in-arms and his freedom. After emerging from his incarceration by Emperor Charles V on 15 March 1528, the king addressed a letter[1] to the city fathers of Paris telling them of his intention "henceforth to spend most of [his] time and to make [his] abode in [his] good city of Paris and the surrounding area rather than elsewhere in his kingdom". This was a political statement, demonstrating the king's intention to take affairs of State seriously from that time forth, and to cut down on his festivities and hunting parties in the Loire valley, where the Valois kings had withdrawn after losing control of the capital during the Hundred Years War.

Francis I had no intention of leading a sedentary existence for all that. After all, French kings had traditionally been nomadic. A day-by-day account exists of Francis I's timetable, and three-quarters of his reign was spent travelling from one place to the next. To demonstrate to his kingdom that he was a free and fit man, Francis I set out on a particularly lengthy tour of France from 1531 to 1534, years that were crucial to the creation of the château of Fontainebleau. In terms of the number of days, he kept his promise to the Parisians: between 1515 and 1524 Francis I spent twenty-eight months in the Loire Valley and thirty-eight in the Île-de-France, while between 1527 and 1547 he spent 112 months in the Île-de-France and twenty-two in the Loire valley. In his letter the king actually specified

Portrait of Francis I by Jean Clouet

This formal portrait intended for Fontainebleau was painted c. 1535. Jean Clouet, painter to the king, was the creator of the French court portrait. Most of his output consists of drawings depicting the main personalities at the Valois court.

that he would take up residence at the Louvre. In fact he contented himself with having the big keep demolished immediately, and it was only in the final years of his reign that he appointed the architect who was to turn the Louvre into a modern residence.

More than his "good city" it was the surrounding areas that benefited from the resolutions spelt out in the royal statement. In the twenty years between his return to Paris (1527) and his death (1547) Francis I built seven châteaux in or near the Île-de-France. Most of them are depicted in the Galerie des Cerfs at Fontainebleau. They fall into two categories, hunting châteaux and royal residences. The hunting châteaux such as La Muette at Saint-Germain-en-Laye or Madrid in the Bois de Boulogne were built quickly on new sites and designed for short stays. Unusual and flimsy, they had no precedent and almost all of them have disappeared. The residences, Saint-Germain-en-Laye and Fontainebleau foremost among them, survived. This was perhaps because of their huge size, designed to accommodate the whole court, and because they had developed around older sites, a guarantee that they would endure. However, the residences that attracted the king and court most were located in huge, game-filled forests, just like the hunting châteaux. "This court is not constituted like other courts," the Duke of Tuscany's ambassador to the French king wrote to his master. "All they think of here is hunting, ladies, festivities and moving on from one place to the next."[2]

Francis I preferred Fontainebleau to all his other residences. There are two important witnesses to this preference: Benvenuto Cellini, the famous goldsmith and sculptor who worked for the king, who reported, "It was, he said, the place in his kingdom where he most enjoyed being"[3], and Jacques Androuet Du Cerceau. In *Les Plus Excellents Bastiments de France* (1576–1579), a collection of plates depicting the most noteworthy châteaux of the sixteenth century, in particular Fontainebleau, he described that the king "liked being there enormously, to such an extent that for the greater part of the time he stayed there [...]. Anything excellent he could find was for his Fontainebleau where he enjoyed being so much that when he wished to go there he said he was going home".

It was the forest that attracted Francis I to Fontainebleau. One of the largest forests at the time in the Île-de-France and now the largest, it still covers the same surface area as it did in the sixteenth century (17,000 hectares), although its vegetation has become denser. "The soil is just sand so the trees in that forest are not normally a good size," Androuet Du Cerceau wrote. But large trees did develop there: the *Jupiter* is a 600-year-old, 35-metre oak which witnessed Francis I's packs of hounds. The forest landscape has not altered much; ferns grow in the outcrops of sandstone and sand, and heather and legends flourish, for example the legend of the white hind, the legend of the master of the royal hunt or the black huntsman whom Francis I met. The large rocks there provided the first men with shelter and supplied building material for the château. There is still game in the forest, but wolves and lynxes disappeared in the nineteenth century.

Exploitation of both game and timber, the two main resources of the forest, was supervised closely in Francis I's reign. Unless they had permission, private citizens were not allowed to hunt in any of the royal forests. In accordance with the decree issued in 1516 a repeat offence could entail the death penalty for the poacher. Cutting wood, a strategically important material, was also the subject of several royal decrees since future shortages of it were beginning to be feared at that time. As far as the forest of Fontainebleau was concerned, Francis I had its boundaries marked (1,000 boundary posts could still be counted in 1977).

In a forest where there are relatively few sources of water the gully formed by the Avon was an ideal site for a residence. Legend has it that one day a dog called Bliaud found the source of the stream, so giving the site its name of Fontainebleau. Now it is thought that there really was a Bliaud, but that he was a forester who had his house in the valley, south of the stream which flows from east to west. On the north bank the kings of France had installed a "palais" a long time ago.

Two charters issued by Louis VII dated 1137 were signed at this place described as a "palais", a word used to describe an important dwelling-place. Louis VII did not leave the French a great deal to remember him by, but some people will recall that he married Eleanor of Aquitaine and, in discarding her, gave his rival, Henry II of England, a wife with great possessions, greatly harming the kingdom of France. The foundation of the palace and the building of the keep at Fontainebleau, still standing today, are attributed to Louis VII. In 1169 he created a chaplain's office there and the Saint-Saturnin chapel. The chapel was consecrated by Thomas à Becket, Archbishop of Canterbury, exiled because of his opposition to policies of King Henry II of England.

Fontainebleau was one of the favourite residences of Louis IX, or St Louis, who signed many acts there. In 1259 he founded a Trinitarian monastery close to the palace, giving it the chapel of Saint-Saturnin, the chaplain's house and his revenue. The Trinitarian order – known in France as the Mathurins – was an order of hospitallers founded in the twelfth century to pay the ransom of Christians captured by the infidel. During the Crusade Louis IX had formed a favourable opinion of their devotion. Communities of the order consisted of seven members at most – the superior, three clerics and three lay brothers – and the monastic buildings had to include a small hospital. Modest as it was, the foundation of this monastery at Fontainebleau was to have important consequences for the way the château evolved; from the sixteenth century it was to encompass the buildings and lands that had belonged to the Mathurins.

A letter from the Dauphin, soon to become King Charles VII, reveals that his mother, Isabeau of Bavaria, who owned the château as part of her widow's dower, had arranged to have it rebuilt[4]. The letter is astonishing for its time, 1431, and its form of address, "Dear lady mother". In the calamitous Treaty of Troyes of 1430 Isabeau had recognised the king of England as ruler of France, so disinheriting her legitimate son (whose legitimacy was openly doubted). The Dauphin was in the Loire valley preparing his revenge and the reconquest of Paris. He describes the rebuilt castle as a "very fine and noteworthy house", its site as a place where the kings had "often been accustomed to enjoy themselves hunting". The house which was perfunctorily fortified had the advantage of being isolated, yet was still close to Paris. "The kings sometimes withdrew there as to a place of solitude," Androuet Du Cerceau commented. On several occasions it was also used as a place of refuge during epidemics.

When Francis I started to take an interest in the château of Fontainebleau, it was "in a tumble-down state". Instead of razing it to the ground he chose to rebuild it, reusing whatever could be reused. The buildings round the Cour Ovale were established on the irregular polygonal outlines, vaguely oval in shape, of the medieval castle. Although he did not drive the monks out, Francis I bought back the Mathurins' demesne: "Since we have made up our mind hereafter to make it our residence for the majority of the time, and to take pleasure in the place and enjoy the hunting of russet and black-haired animals."[5]

Work started in August 1527, just three months after the King's solemn entry into Paris on 14 April, not at the château but at the monastery where the masons had to work "in great haste day and night" in anticipation of the arrival of the king and his mother, Louise of Savoy[6]. The monastery, which had been continuously lived in by the monks, was no doubt in a better state than the castle to provide temporary accommodation after repairs and enlargements, and gave the king time to finalise his intentions and have them recorded by his master mason, Gilles Le Breton, in the 1528 "devis" – the key item in the history of the château.

In the sixteenth century a "devis" was the description of the work to be done, or a specification, and was distinct from the contract that committed the craftsman to carry out the work. This 1528 specification, which covers twenty printed pages in the nineteenth-century publication, *Comptes des bâtiments du roi* [7], is complex. To encourage the reader to be indulgent towards historians who may have misconstrued the text, one of its forty articles is directly quoted here – the reader is not expected to understand it: "*Item.* A large wall must be built to separate the said pavilion from the said lodging of my said lords my children, at the side of the said three blocks of houses aforementioned, which large wall will be four feet thick at its foundations and three feet thick from the ground floor up to the coping", etc.[8]

According to our reading of this specification it seems that from 1527 to about 1535 the master builder had no lesser task than "to rebuild anew the buildings that are at present falling down", and between the castle to the east and the monastery to the west to erect the wing which was to house the Galerie François Premier.

The question of the identity of the architect, or "deviseur", as the writer of the "devis" was called, who directed the work in the 1530s remains unanswered. It may even be that the answer lies in the very words "devis" and "deviseur". Gilles Le Breton, who was to remain in charge of the masonry work throughout the king's reign and beyond, without anyone else sharing his responsibility in the 1530s, was a skilled craftsman who knew his trade. In 1527 he had acquired the office of General Master of the King's Masonry Work, which meant that he was the foremost mason in the kingdom[9]. To carry out the first fairly rough and ready work in accordance with the 1528 specification, detailed as it was in its description of what was required, there was no need for drawings. No doubt he managed without them. The client and the mason produced architecture without an architect, and the "deviseur" was the king himself.

Galerie François Premier

Following pages:
The stucco figures executed between 1535–1537 and the frescoes started in 1536
are the work of Rosso. The decoration of the middle area of the gallery was completed
by Primaticcio. From 1539 Francesco Scibec de Carpi made the wainscoting,
the parquet floor – now gone – and probably the ceiling.

Christine de Pisan said of King Charles V, the pride of the Valois dynasty and Francis I's role model, that he demonstrated his knowledge of architecture "by making specifications for his buildings". Writing about the château of Villers-Cotterêts, Androuet Du Cerceau said that Francis I "was marvellously devoted to buildings and that they were his greatest pleasure, as he also demonstrated in the number of houses he built". With regard to Saint-Germain-en-Laye, Francis I was "so good at understanding building that it could almost be said that he was the sole architect". If Francis I was the architect of Saint-Germain-en-Laye, started in 1539, he could very well have been the architect of Fontainebleau.

When he organised the administration of his buildings in 1528 ,Francis I made his manservant, Florimond de Champverne, the repository of his ideas: "We give power and authority to the said de Champverne to conduct, specify, make and perfect the said building and construction of Fontainebleau," the king wrote. Some believe that de Champverne was the architect of the château[10]. It is probable that he was no more than the permanent on-site representative of the king.

In the background there is a figure who may have played an important role because of his professional skills. Pierre Paule, or Paulle, known as The Italian, was described on the occasion of some completed work in 1528 as "architect, manservant to Madame, and keeper of the château of Moulins"[11]. He shared the role of supervisor with Pierre Des Hôtels. The supervisor ensured that the work had been carried out properly, i.e. checked that the terms of the specifications and contracts had been respected. Pierre Paule supervised the work until his death on 28 December 1535[12]. He was buried in the chapel of the Ave Maria monastery in Paris. On his tombstone the inscription read: "Here lies the noble man Master Pierre Paulle known as The Italian, architect to our lord the king, manservant in ordinary to the said lord, controller of his buildings and his keeper at the châteaux of Fontainebleau, Moulins and Bourbon-l'Archambault"[13]. Being keeper, or "concierge", meant being governor, so he was by no means a lowly person.

Pierre Paule was there throughout the course of the first stage of work, and although he was only the controller, this did not prevent him from making a contribution to the design. He may even have been an intermediary between the king and the mason, an interpreter capable of producing drawings for the most important areas. He had been architect to Madame, or Louise of Savoy. It was she who saved the kingdom when the king was held prisoner, and it was Louise who had such a powerful influence over her son, who was full of respect for her that he gave up the bedroom on the first floor of the keep for her, the room being traditionally reserved for the king. As a result of the proceedings brought by Francis I against

Charles of Bourbon, Louise became heir to the Bourbonnais, the châteaux of Moulins and Bourbon-l'Archambault in particular. Pierre Paule was thus a member of Louise's staff and she passed him on to the king.[14] On the death of Louise of Savoy in 1531 and that of Pierre Paule in 1535, the painters and sculptors could set to work on the newly rebuilt château and the gallery linking it to the monastery, which had also been rebuilt.

In 1530 Giovanni Battista di Jacopo, known as Rosso Fiorentino, the red-headed Florentine, arrived at Fontainebleau, and in 1532 Francesco Primaticcio, known as Bologna after his native town, followed. Fontainebleau was to be the scene of veiled rivalry, even overt opposition, between artists from two different regions of Italy: the Tuscans/Florentines versus the Bolognese/Emilians/Lombards.

Rosso admired Michelangelo, the eminent Florentine artist who had placed Florence at the forefront of the artistic scene in Italy. Francis I had tried to persuade him to come to France, but to no avail. Only Michelangelo could have filled the space left by the death of another great Florentine, Leonardo da Vinci, in the Loire valley in 1519. Rosso had worked with Perino del Vaga and Parmigianino in Rome and had had to flee in 1527 when Rome was sacked by Emperor Charles V's troops. The sacking of Rome was a major event in the political history of Europe, destroying the illusions of the Renaissance, but it was beneficial in terms of Francis I's artistic policy, enabling him to find men who would never have left Rome. After 1527 Rosso led an itinerant life. In 1530 he was in Venice as the guest of Aretino who recommended him to Francis I, sending him a drawing by Rosso, *Mars and Venus*, now in the Louvre. Rosso's major work was the decoration of the gallery described in the 1528 specification. It seems that the decoration did not start before 1535. So what did Rosso do during the first five years he spent in France? No doubt he was busy assembling the large portfolio of drawings that had to be produced before a paintbrush was allowed in the gallery. Apart from the *Écouen pietà*, now in the Louvre, no pictures produced by Rosso in France have been preserved. Nonetheless his concepts for the gallery, reproduced in the form of prints, immediately became known throughout Europe, bringing Rosso international acclaim. Francis I admired him, showering benefits upon him, "so much so that Rosso did not live like a painter, but like a prince, with a full household, horses, a dwelling full of tapestries, silver, furniture and ornaments", wrote Vasari in his *Vite de' più eccellenti Pittori, Scultori e Architetti Italiani* (1550).

Mars and Venus

This drawing by Rosso, produced in Venice in 1530 at the request of Aretino and intended for Francis I, is an allegory celebrating the marriage between the king of France and Eleanor of Austria. Rosso used the subject again in a painting – now destroyed – at one end of the Galerie François Premier.

Portrait of Rosso

This portrait was published in Vasari's *Vite de' più eccellenti Pittori, Scultori e Architetti Italiani*, in 1550.

Cleobis and Biton

This tapestry reproducing one of the panels in the Galerie François Premier is part of a set of tapestries woven at Fontainebleau c. 1539–1544, now in the Kunsthistorisches Museum, Vienna.

Portrait of Primaticcio

This portrait was published
in Vasari's *Vite de' più
eccellenti Pittori, Scultori
e Architetti Italiani*, in 1568.

Rosso was the founder of what has come to be known as the School of
Fontainebleau, one of the branches of European Mannerism. He died prematurely
in 1540, mourned as sorely by the king as Leonardo had been.

In spite of his parochial outlook, Vasari – a Florentine – devoted an entry in
the second edition of his *Vite* (1568) to Primaticcio, one of the few living artists
to be so honoured. Primaticcio was eight years younger than Rosso and lived thirty
years after him, occupying the foremost place at Fontainebleau from the time of
Rosso's death until his own. Francis I had made an offer to Giulio Romano who
was busy creating the Palazzo del Te for the Duke of Mantua, a strange residence
which was the talk of all the courts of Europe. Romano refused it, but sent him
Primaticcio, who had been working at the Palazzo del Te as a stucco artist; some
hint that Giulio Romano was not sorry to be rid of a young pupil whose talent was
beginning to outshine his own.

Primaticcio was soon given a prestigious commission and entrusted with the
decoration of the royal apartments, albeit presenting himself as the interpreter of
Giulio Romano's ideas. The décor of the king's bedchamber in the keep, carried
out during 1535–1536 is now only known through a drawing by Primaticcio after
Giulio Romano. Of Queen Eleanor's bedchamber (Emperor Charles V's sister, and
Francis I's second wife), only the chimney-piece has been preserved: the central
painting is again executed after a drawing by Giulio Romano, but the development

Story of Psyche

This proposal for the decoration of the royal bedchamber in the Keep was drawn in 1532
by Primaticcio, then a young man newly arrived from Mantua, and still under the influence
of his master Giulio Romano, to whom the drawing was long attributed.
Primaticcio probably took his inspiration from a composition by Giulio Romano.
The decoration was executed after this drawing was destroyed, so we do not know if
the terminal figures were to be treated as frescoes or in stucco. If they were in stucco,
this would mean Primaticcio introduced high-relief stucco work to Fontainebleau,
a technique widely used by Rosso in the Galerie François Premier.

of the frame, treated in high-relief stucco, is an innovation regarded for some years
as the most original decorative feature at Fontainebleau. Paintings set in stucco
frameworks had been seen elsewhere, particularly at the Palazzo del Te, but both
in surface and relief the stucco had been no more than a foil for the picture. In the
queen's bedchamber Primaticcio pushed the technique, for which he had been
summoned to Fontainebleau, to new limits in order to make his mark alongside
his Florentine rival. But the decoration of the queen's bedchamber (1534–1537)
coincided with the first work carried out in the gallery where, it seems, Primaticcio did not collaborate with Rosso. Thus Rosso was the instigator of the generous
stucco frames in the gallery, meaning that it is no longer clear as to which of the
two artists can take credit for the innovation. Primaticcio would be the favourite
contender if it could be verified that the canephora terms in the king's bedchamber, seen only in the drawing, were made of stucco.

By the end of the 1530s Francis I may have felt that the transformation of
the château of Fontainebleau was complete. To allow him to witness the success
of the venture, he invited his former gaoler Charles V to Fontainebleau, where he
stayed from 24 to 30 December 1539. A strange visit indeed! The meeting of the

Chimney-piece in Queen Eleanor's bedchamber, now Salon François Premier

All that remains of the decoration of the bedchamber of Eleanor of Austria,
Emperor Charles V's sister, whom Francis I married in 1530, is the fire-place canopy.
It had been decorated with stucco figures and a fresco by Primaticcio between 1534 and 1537.
The high-relief stuccos were among the first to be made at Fontainebleau. The central fresco
depicting Venus and Adonis was executed after a drawing by Giulio Romano.

two sovereigns at Aigues-Mortes had just put an end to one of their most violent
clashes. The emperor had gained permission to travel across France to castigate
his rebelling Flemish subjects, fearing for his safety if he travelled by sea. In the
cities he was met with triumphal arches; Rosso was approached to design the
entrance into Paris. Unfortunately the drawings he made have been lost, but his
involvement presupposes an aptitude for architectural drawing. In fact Rosso did
no more than draw up an idea which came from the king: a large Hercules
supporting two columns, symbolising the empire where the sun never set[15].
There is a written account of the emperor's reception at Fontainebleau:

*The king was very keen to show the emperor his fine house which he
had built at Fontainebleau, a very attractive place because of the*

Bedchamber of the Duchess of Étampes

Apelles painting Alexander and Campaspe

The bedroom of Francis I's mistress, subsequently very much altered, was decorated by Primaticcio in 1541–1544 with scenes depicting Alexander with women, in a reference to Francis I's love life. In 1834 the painters Charles Moench and Alexandre Abel de Pujol attempted to restore the original composition, using sixteenth-century engravings after Primaticcio. Only the wall seen in the photograph has preserved its original decoration intact: above the door, *Alexander taming the horse Bucephalus*, on the large fresco, *The Marriage of Alexander and Roxana*.

This engraving with the monogram "LD" was made after Primaticcio's fresco – now destroyed – for the bedroom of the Duchess of Étampes, who gave him her constant protection. The engraving, typical of the School of Fontainebleau, was used as a model for reinstating the decoration in the nineteenth century. The subject is disturbingly ambiguous, and can be interpreted as a painting of the king and his mistress. At the time many people would have remembered how Alexander had given up Campaspe to the painter Apelles who had fallen in love with her.

*large forests surrounding the house where there is excellent hunting
because of the large number of wild animals, russet, black and other
colours, which live in these forests because of their size. This house is
also surrounded by beautiful stretches of water, fountains, and
fish-ponds as well as several other fine and agreeable things which
the king greatly loves and which entice him so often. The said place is
situated outside Paris, at a distance of about fourteen or fifteen leagues.
The king took the emperor there on his way to Paris, even though it
was not on their route, because of his great desire to show him his house
where he likes so much to stay on account of its beauty.* (16)

That visit closes the first decade of the Fontainebleau Renaissance. The 1540 Edict
of Fontainebleau marked the beginning of a new decade: the period of tolerance
was over, and Francis I chose repression as the means for dealing with those of his
subjects who supported the Reformation.

The painters celebrated the defender of the orthodox faith, and a century later
a second Edict of Fontainebleau was to deprive the Protestants of the freedoms
accorded to them by Henri IV.

Commodus Hercules, Apollo Belvedere and the Ariadne of the Vatican

Now in the Galerie des Cerfs, these three bronzes after antique statues
in the Vatican were cast, on Francis I's instructions, in 1541–1543 from moulds made in
Rome by Primaticcio in 1540.

In February 1540 Francis I sent Primaticcio to Rome to buy antiquities on his behalf, or to have moulds of the most famous ones made. On Rosso's death (14 November 1540) Primaticcio immediately returned to take up the leading position at Fontainebleau. He brought back the moulds, and used them to cast superb bronzes which contributed to the renown of Francis I's château. It was this addition which led someone to tell Vasari that Fontainebleau had become a "new Rome". There is no point listing the bronzes in detail; they were in any case supplemented by later trips and curtailed by a few that went missing. Only the *Ariadne of the Vatican* (at the time identified as Cleopatra), the *Laocoön*, the *Apollo Belvedere*, the *Cnidian Venus* and the *Commodus Hercules* are worth mentioning, the most famous statues in the Vatican collections; these bronzes have fortunately been preserved at Fontainebleau. *The Tiber*, also copied from the Vatican collections, disappeared after giving its name to a flowerbed in the Grand Jardin. The bronze copies of the two satyrs from the Palazzo della Valle which adorned the chimney-piece in the Salle de Bal were melted down at the time of the Revolution, but replaced in 1960. Only a plaster cast was made of Marcus Aurelius's horse at the Capitol, and for a long time it adorned the servants' courtyard, which became known as the Cour du Cheval Blanc.

It took more than the installation of the sculpture of a horse, however, to turn a servants' courtyard into the main court of the château. Francis I realised that the exterior of Fontainebleau failed to live up to the interior, and that it was time (if not too late) to endow his château with the regularity that was regarded at the time as the epitome of modernity. He turned to Sebastiano Serlio, one of Italy's famous architects, and the first architect of such stature to be employed at Fontainebleau.

Serlio was already an old man and he had attracted attention not through the buildings he had created but through the publication of important treatises. In the century when printing had made ideas available to all, and architecture – not to be confused with construction – was defined as the art of specification through drawings or words, publishing written works was considered far more prestigious than constructing buildings. What was needed to halt the haphazard development of the royal château was a mind not unbound by material considerations.

Serlio was one of the artists who fled from Rome when it was sacked. Along with Peruzzi he had recorded a great many antique monuments and published his drawings under the title *Le antiquita di Roma* (Venice, 1540), dedicating the book to Francis I. He had previously sent to the king a copy of his first publication, *Regole generali di architettura* (Venice, 1537). The fact that the two treatises were designated as Book IV and Book III, numbered inversely to the order in which they appeared, indicated a coherent and far-reaching programme. Books I and II were published in Paris in 1545, Book V likewise in Paris in 1547; the *Libro extraordinario* in Lyon in 1551. Books VI to VIII were published posthumously – Serlio died in 1554.

Georges d'Armagnac, Bishop of Rodez, the king's ambassador to Venice, had opened the way which led Sebastiano to the king. As early as 1539 Francis I had responded to receiving the copy of Book IV with a gift of 300 gold crowns and a proposal to appoint Serlio the "*Generale sopra le fabriche regie*" (Superintendent of the Royal Buildings). In the preface to Book III Serlio had expressed a desire to come and study the antiquities of southern France. He arrived at Fontainebleau in late 1540 or early 1541[17]. Letters patent dated 27 December 1541 establish Serlio's payment, which was "based on his said position as painter and architect in ordinary with regard to his [the king's] buildings and constructions at the site of Fontainebleau"[18]. A perceptible shift in title can be detected: Serlio is also described as a painter but his field of activity is confined to Fontainebleau, at least so it would seem (the text "at Fontainebleau", but not exclusively Fontainebleau). This did not prevent Serlio from coming up with a design for the Louvre, although Pierre Lescot's was chosen in preference.

This setback and uncertainties as to Serlio's title have given credence to the suggestion that Serlio did nothing at Fontainebleau. Although this opinion has been adopted by historians, Part Two will revert to the beliefs expressed by those who chronicled events at the château: Father Dan, author of the *Trésor des Merveilles de la Maison royale de Fontainebleau* (1642), and the Abbé Guilbert, author of the *Description du château, bourg et forêt de Fontainebleau* (1731), who attributed a fair number of the château buildings to Serlio. At the very least, it is worth pointing out now that Serlio was behind the first attempt to bring regularity to the buildings. He was no more able than someone like Pierre Paule to dispense with an intrinsically French site architect, in this case Pierre Chambiges, who had just started work on rebuilding the château of Saint-Germain-en-Laye.

Did Primaticcio, who was in Italy in 1540, play a part in arranging for Serlio, also from Bologna, to come to France? Who knows, but his arrival certainly strengthened the Bolognese camp. On the Florentine side Benvenuto Cellini had just appeared on the scene, a powerful goldsmith, sculptor, swashbuckler and braggart, quick to defend the outstanding reputation of Florence, as well as his own. The memoirs he wrote are no less full of incident than the most picaresque of novels.

Cellini arrived at Fontainebleau in 1540 ready to take on the mantle of Rosso, "our famous Florentine painter with his extraordinary talent"[19]. He did not spare Serlio, even though they were not competing on the same ground, and accused him of pinching the antiquities he had published from Peruzzi. His prime target, however, was obviously Primaticcio: "All the best things he did were inspired by the admirable style of my compatriot who had died shortly before"[20]. In Cellini's account it is hard to distinguish between personal rivalry and national animosity. When he tried to be conciliatory, Primaticcio was accused by Cellini of deceiving him "with Lombard-style compliments".

Following is Cellini's irresistible story about the Jupiter which was to be brought face to face with Primaticcio's antique statues in the gallery. Primaticcio was supported by the Duchess of Étampes, the king's mistress, whom Cellini had not succeeded in winning over:

> *I finished my fine silver Jupiter with the utmost care and brought it to Fontainebleau where the king was in residence. Primaticcio had brought back his statues from Rome and had had them carefully cast in bronze. I knew nothing about this because he had conducted the operation in great secrecy;*

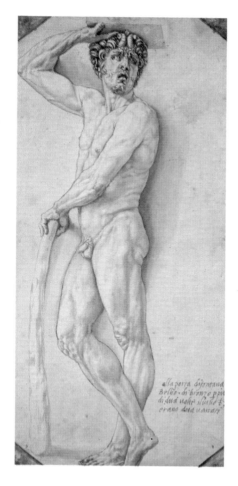

Decoration for the Porte Dorée

The decoration commissioned by
Cellini for the Porte Dorée,
the main entrance to the château,
was to consist of a tympanum adorned
with the nymph of Fontainebleau,
two spandrels adorned with Victories,
and two piers in the form of satyrs.
The maquette of the doorway was
submitted to Francis I in 1543.
The tympanum (1542–1545) and
the spandrels (1544–1545) were made,
but never installed at Fontainebleau.
Henri II gave them to Diane de Poitiers
for Anet. Today, the two spandrels are
known only through plaster versions;
the tympanum is now at the Louvre;
and there is only known to be a drawing
of the satyrs, which is in Washington
in the Woodner Collection.

moreover Fontainebleau is forty miles from Paris and it was not
possible to know what was happening there. I asked the king
where he wanted to put the Jupiter. Madame d'Étampes was
present and said to him there was nowhere more suitable than
his fine gallery. This gallery, a hundred feet long and twelve
feet wide, was embellished by paintings by our wonderful
compatriot Rosso. Bologna had set up his antique statues
there. As I have already said, they were the finest things that
could be reproduced from among the antiquities of Rome.
I had my Jupiter carried there. When I saw the skilful
arrangement, I said to myself: "It's as if I had to pass between
a double row of pikes! May God help me!" I put my statue in
its place, arranged it to the best possible advantage and awaited
the great king's arrival. Jupiter carried his thunderbolt in his
right hand, as if he was about to throw it, and in his left the
earth's globe. Amidst the flames of the thunderbolt I had

*skilfully concealed a short white wax torch. Madame
d'Étampes had delayed the king until the evening to spite me:
either the king would not come at all or if he came my work
would not show to advantage in the dark. Thanks to God who
protects those who put their trust in him, the very opposite
happened: seeing that it was getting dark, I lit the torch which
was a little above the god's head and the light, coming from above,
made a far finer effect than daylight. The king arrived with
Madame d'Étampes and immediately declared: "Nobody has
ever seen anything as fine. Even I who love and appreciate art
would never have imagined anything a hundredth as splendid."
Madame d'Étampes had the cheek to exclaim: "Have you no eyes?
Don't you see all the fine figures of antique bronzes over there?
That is where sculptural perfection lies, not in these modern
idiocies!" The king stepped forward, the others behind him, and
took a look at the copies by Bologna; they were poorly lit, and
did not look their best. "Whoever wanted to put this man at a
disadvantage," he said, "has done him a proud service. The
comparison with these superb statues proves that his is more
beautiful still. We must sing Benvenuto's praises since his*

Salt cellar by Benvenuto Cellini

This remarkable example of the goldsmith's art made for Francis I by Cellini in 1540–1543
is today in the Kunsthistorisches Museum, Vienna.

*works can withstand being shown face to face with antique
ones, and even surpass them." Madame d'Étampes remarked
that my statue would appear a thousand times less beautiful in
the daylight than it did at night; and account must also be taken
of the fact I had placed a veil over it to hide its faults. The veil in
question was a very light one I had elegantly draped over my
Jupiter to enhance its majesty. Upon these words I took hold of it,
raised it and in so doing uncovered the fine virile member of
the god, and in a gesture obviously betraying my irritation I tore
it up. Madame d'Étampes thought I had uncovered that part
of the statue to embarrass her and the king noticed her annoyance.*

No longer controlling my anger I wanted to speak, but the king
in his wisdom got in before me, and speaking in French said
word for word: "Benvenuto, say nothing; if you keep quiet
you will receive a thousand times more than you wish."(21)

The statue of Jupiter has disappeared; the Fontainebleau nymph that Cellini intended for the Porte Dorée is in the Louvre and his famous golden salt cellar is in Vienna. There is nothing left at Fontainebleau to recall his presence there.

Other Italian artists passed through Fontainebleau, and although they did not attract as much attention, they were fine artists nonetheless. Among those from Florence or Tuscany was the painter Luca Penni, who arrived in France c. 1530, collaborated with Rosso in the gallery, left in 1540, a date that marked a turning-point, and worked in Paris where he died in 1556; the sculptor Domenico del Barbiere, known as Domenico Fiorentino, who arrived at Fontainebleau in Rosso's wake, but worked with Primaticcio after 1540; and the sculptor and ceramicist Giralomo della Robbia who had been in France as early as 1518, working mainly at the château of Madrid, and who was commissioned to make a ceramic work for Fontainebleau, though it may never have been made.

As far as the Bolognese/Emilians were concerned, there were Giacomo Barozzi da Vignola, not famous at that point, who seems to have stayed in France from 1541 to just 1543 to assist Primaticcio in the casting of the antique statues; and Francesco Scibec de Carpi, a joiner or ornamental sculptor, who was responsible for the most remarkable works in this specialist area made in the reigns of Francis I or Henri II – he must have arrived in France before 1531 because he was the executor of the will of his protector and fellow countryman Alberto Pio, Count of Carpi, a diplomat, humanist and personal friend of Francis I who died in 1531.(22) The arrival in France of the painters Nicolò dell'Abate and Ruggiero de Ruggieri, who were among Primaticcio's main collaborators, was subsequent to the reign of Francis I.

From Henri II to Henry IV

*Henri II's reign, the Pléiade • The painters active at Fontainebleau
in the second half of the sixteenth century, Nicolò dell'Abate, Caron, Cousin,
the Clouets • De l'Orme in the service of Henri II • The last Valois kings •
Henri IV • the Francinis and the gardens, Matthieu Jacquet and the Belle
Cheminée • The painters Dubreuil, Fréminet and Dubois*

Henri II, Francis II, Charles IX, Henri III, Henri IV: who now knows the order of succession? Only the reigns of Henri II and Henri IV, and to a lesser extent that of Charles IX, are important in the story of Fontainebleau. Francis II did not live long, and Henri III only lived until the civil war which, in the end, took his life.

Henri II's reign itself only lasted just over ten years (1547–1559); if he had lived longer he might have outshone Louis XIV, and the sixteenth rather than the seventeenth century might have been France's "grand siècle". Everything combined to make this reign a major period in French art. At the end of 1547 Joachim Du Bellay met the youthful Ronsard, and from that meeting an association arose that at first adopted the warlike name of the "Brigade" before becoming, after the battle had been fought and almost won, the Pléiade. The *Deffense et illustration de la langue française* (1549) was their manifesto. By preferring the "language of the country, living and flourishing" to the languages of antiquity, "the ashes of the ancients" (Ronsard), they intended to give short shrift to anyone who told them how things should be done, i.e. Italians like Cellini who poked fun at "French bad taste"[1]. The Pléiade were the first exponents of French-style classicism, a movement set up outside Fontainebleau by natives of France, mainly poets, but also sculptors and architects. The painters, when they were not at Fontainebleau, kept to themselves.

The change of guard which seems to be associated with Henri II's accession to the throne may have started during his father's reign, first demonstrated by Francis I's choice of Lescot rather than Serlio to build the new Louvre. But it was in

Door of the Salle de Bal

This was made after a drawing by Philibert De l'Orme, c. 1550.

Henri II's reign that artists such as Lescot, Goujon or De l'Orme created their masterpieces. The change in names was not only seen in the arts, and it was doubtlessly inspired less by a love of the Classical style than by the desire of those close to Henri and Diane de Poitiers to avenge themselves on those surrounding the Duchess of Étampes, Francis I's erstwhile favourite.

Primaticcio, however, did not lose the position he occupied at Fontainebleau even though he had benefited from the duchess's protection. It was during Henri II's reign that most of the work on his two main achievements, the Salle de Bal and the Galerie d'Ulysse (destroyed), was carried out. To bring such a mammoth task to a successful conclusion, he introduced more Emilians into his team. On his advice in 1552, Henri II sent for Nicolò dell'Abate, a painter of proven talent. Nicolò is said to have coloured in the drawings that Primaticcio prepared for the Salle de Bal and the gallery; in other words it was the second-in-command rather than the master who was seen on the scaffolding with a brush in his hand. Nicolò left Fontainebleau at the same time as Primaticcio.

The first mention in France of Ruggiero de Ruggieri, described by Vasari as a pupil of Primaticcio who was active in Bologna, does not occur until 1557. His major work at Fontainebleau, the *Vie d'Hercule* in the Pavillon des Poêles, has disappeared. Among noteworthy painters, Antoine Caron was the only Frenchman to have worked at Fontainebleau. From 1561 he stopped working as one of the Fontainebleau team, but he kept their Italianate style. He then devoted himself to depicting events of the day, often in allegorical form. *Les Massacres du Triumvirate* painted in 1566 is a clear reference to the atrocities of the period (the massacre of the Protestants at Wassy in 1562). In place of the triumvirate composed of Octavius Caesar, Anthony and Lepidus, Guise, Montmorency and Saint-André, who had formed an alliance to fight the Protestants, can be recognised. Caron also produced the drawings on which the cartoons for the *Fêtes des Valois* tapestries were based, illustrating royal festivities during the reign of Charles IX, in particular one that took place on the Étang at Fontainebleau in 1564[2]. In this, Greeks and Trojans confront one another in a sinister simulacrum of the fight between the Catholics and Protestants at the wedding of the king's sister Marguerite to Henri de Bourbon, the future Henri IV – a prelude to the St. Bartholomew's Day massacres.

The most prolific and highly regarded French painters, Jean Cousin the Elder and Younger, were influenced by Fontainebleau, but never worked there. Jean Clouet and his son François who specialised in court portraits were even more remote from it. Confronted with the large Italian workforce operating at full tilt in Fontainebleau, it was very hard for a French school of painting to gain a

Portraits of Henri II and Charles IX by the studio of François Clouet

These portraits – now in the Louvre – executed in the studios of the Clouets
who specialised in court portraiture were produced in more than one copy. Where Charles IX
is concerned, a 1561 head-and-shoulders portrait is known to exist as well as the original of the
full-length portrait dating from c. 1566, both by François Clouet.

The Massacres perpetrated by the Triumvirate by Antoine Caron

This picture painted in 1566 – today in the Louvre – depicting the massacres
carried out in Rome by the triumvirate of Octavius Caesar, Mark Anthony
and Lepidus recalls the action against the Protestants taken by Montmorency, Guise and
Saint-André. The massacre of Wassy had taken place in 1562. Several Roman monuments can
be recognised in the picture, including the *Apollo Belvedere* and the *Commodus Hercules*, two
of the antique statues which Primaticcio had taken moulds of on Francis I's instructions, in
the foreground (p. 26). Caron worked at Fontainebleau alongside Primaticcio and Nicolò
dell'Abate. A distinguished representative of the School of Fontainebleau, he specialised
in allegorically depicting the events of his day.

foothold. For sculpture the situation was different. The fact that the outstanding
representatives of the French contingent were not working at Fontainebleau can be
explained by the fact that their achievements were taking shape elsewhere, in
particular at the Louvre: perhaps this was because Fontainebleau was dominated
by a powerful, authoritarian architect, Philibert De l'Orme, who had surrounded
himself with Frenchmen, but ones of little renown.

At Fontainebleau it was really only in architecture that there was a change-
over. The appointment of De l'Orme, who had been Henri's architect when he was
Dauphin, as Architect to the King led to the departure of Serlio, who left
Fontainebleau for Lyon in 1547. At an unknown date (he must still have been in

Water festivity at Fontainebleau

The *Valois tapestries* depicting court festivities – of which this example now at the Uffizi
in Florence is part – were executed c. 1588, based on cartoons by Lucas de Heere and inspired
by Antoine Caron's drawings. Caron's drawings depict festivities held in Charles IX's reign, but the
cartoons were made to glorify Henri III, shown here in the company
of Queen Louise. Caron's original drawing (Edinburgh, National Gallery of Scotland)
probably represents the festivity held on the Étang in 1564, in which Greeks and Trojans come
face to face. The representation of the château is very fanciful.

Lyon in 1551 to publish his *Libro extraordinario* there) he returned to Fontainebleau where he died in 1554. His return may have been motivated by the hope of pushing through his scheme for a loggia, known by the posthumous publication of Book VII (Frankfurt-am-Main, 1575). De l'Orme was looking for ways of saving the Salle de Bal wing, which had been badly built by Le Breton. It may have seemed a good opportunity to get a rival scheme accepted, but Serlio had no chance against De l'Orme. He courteously applauded the intervention of this "man of authority" who in this matter showed "more judgement than the mason who had put up the building", but that did not prevent him from adding bitterly: "Yet I who was there, living there continually, paid by the magnanimity of King Francis, was not asked for the least bit of advice: *nè mi fù pur dimandato un minimo consiglio*"[3]. This complaint is clearly from a very old man, close to death, who had lost his place to an ambitious young man. It is a mistake to date this admission of failure to the 1540s when Serlio was the only architect at Fontainebleau. It is worth noting that the rivalry between the two men did not rule out mutual esteem. Serlio's praise of the "man of authority" was matched in De l'Orme's treatise[4] by this tribute to Serlio: "He was the first person to give the French through his books and drawings some knowledge of antique buildings and of several very fine innovations, and I knew him as a good and kindly man."

The final years of Francis I's reign had encouraged a certain slackness, a weakening of control. On 3 April 1548 Henri II, "wanting to know and understand how the late king [...] was served in his buildings [...] whether there have not been any malpractices or abuses", gave De l'Orme the commission of inspecting the main royal building sites, including Fontainebleau[5]. Such commissions were traditionally entrusted to great lords, and by accumulating them De l'Orme became the first French architect to take on the role of Superintendent of Buildings. His powers were limited only by the exclusion of the Louvre from the scope of his authority, and at Fontainebleau by the supremacy Primaticcio still exercised over painting.

At Fontainebleau the inspection revealed major cases of negligence, imperilling the preservation of the buildings, and of overcharging, blame for which

The organ loft of the upper Saint-Saturnin chapel

Saint-Saturnin chapel, built by Francis I, was embellished in Henri II's reign by the addition of an organ loft, designed by Philibert De l'Orme and made by Francesco Scibec de Carpi in 1554. All that remains of it are the two Ionic columns and a piece of flooring bearing this inscription on the frieze: "*Henricus II dei gratia francorum rex christianissimus*".

Portrait of Philibert De l'Orme

This anonymous portrait
of the famous architect (1514–1570)
who worked at Fontainebleau
in the reign of Henri II was published
in 1576 in a second posthumous
edition of his treatise on architecture.

Ceiling of bedchamber of Henri II

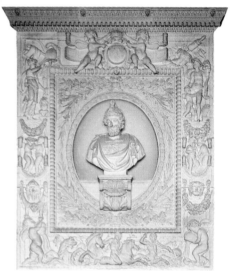

Chimney-piece in the bedchamber of Henri II

The front of the canopy was commissioned by the sculptor Pierre Bontemps in 1555: it is supposed to depict the "four stages of the year", but only two of the seasons can be identified. The central oval was decorated with a painting by Nicolò dell'Abate probably depicting *Diana and Venus* (the subject is indicated by Father Dan, who attributes the painting to Toussaint Dubreuil). In the twentieth century the front was remounted in the hybrid chimney-piece in the Salle des Gardes, with a bust of Henri IV replacing the painting.

Of the bedchamber made for Henri II in the Pavillon des Poêles following Philibert De l'Orme's designs, only the ceiling and the front of the fireplace canopy remain. The sculptor Ambroise Perret was commissioned to execute the ceiling in 1558. It is adorned with the figures of the seven planets; not the heavens according to Copernicus, but the heavens of antiquity in which the sun was a planet. The ceiling was reused in the Queen-Mothers' Apartment, and Henri II's cipher was replaced by Anne of Austria's.

Chimney-piece in the Salle de Bal

Made after De l'Orme's design, with the ciphers and symbols of Henri II, this was completed
in 1556. The bronze satyrs are recent copies, replacing Primaticcio's copies
of the antique satyrs in the Palazzo della Valle.

could all be laid at Le Breton's door. De l'Orme's first task was to repair the buildings, but just as Serlio had done, he also developed a grand design for Fontainebleau. His main amendment to the layout involved moving the entrance of the château from the Porte Dorée, opening directly into the Cour Ovale, to the servants' courtyard built on the site of the Couvent des Mathurins, thus promoting it to the rank of a forecourt and court of honour (the Cour du Cheval Blanc). This meant regularising, or at least repairing, the parts that had already been constructed as well as a general change of layout. De l'Orme proposed moving the royal apartment out of the dark Cour Ovale and placing it between the new court of honour and the Cour de la Fontaine, near the Étang. Due to the brevity of Henri II's reign these plans never reached fruition, although the fact that De l'Orme took a greater interest in sites where he had more freedom of manoeuvre, such as Anet for example, was also a contributing factor.

Only fragments remain of De l'Orme's intervention, though they are important fragments and very indicative of the unprecedented expansion of the architect's role. De l'Orme was not a mason, but an accomplished artist who provided design drawings for the decoration. Scibec de Carpi, the only Italian in his team, received drawings of the panelling for the Salle de Bal, the king's apartment and the Trinité church from him. The organ loft at Saint-Saturnin chapel, the ceiling and chimney-piece of the king's bedchamber as well as the chimney-piece in the Salle de Bal bear De l'Orme's signature, and the sculptors did no more than execute his designs. In the Salle de Bal he specified a ceiling, for which a drawing was provided, where Le Breton had constructed a barrel vault. All these represented areas which had been taken away from the painter's control. It has been said that Primaticcio himself had wished for such a change, but this seems unlikely since Primaticcio would have been quite capable of bringing Le Breton round to his point of view before De l'Orme appeared on the scene. One of the consequences of the new way in which roles were assigned was the disappearance of stucco work. Comparing the Galerie François Premier and the Salle de Bal provides convincing evidence for this theory: the construction of large stucco pieces could only be conceived within a framework where the painter controlled the decoration.

The king's accidental death in 1559 changed the course of destiny. De l'Orme, who had made many enemies in exercising his authority, was replaced as superintendent by Primaticcio, with the support of the Guise family, who were very powerful during the reign of Francis II. Primaticcio had worked in the houses of the Guise family, and because he had designed a grotto for them – at Meudon – the Guises thought that they could turn someone capable of designing a small garden building into the architect of a castle rooted in the past. One can see how Primaticcio demonstrated his skill in two-dimensional architectural drawing when he created the wing of the Belle Cheminée, evident in the elevations and façades. Yet despite his obvious talent for manipulating spaces, he lacked an overall view of the way a large château functioned. In diverting the flow of circulation which De l'Orme had intended to position centrally, he may have had no other intention than to cancel out his predecessor's work. Nonetheless, Primaticcio, assisted by Nicolò dell'Abate, worked almost until his death on the splendid Galerie d'Ulysse, the most accomplished and widely imitated work produced by the School of Fontainebleau.

Apart from the Belle Cheminée wing, Charles IX commissioned two pieces of work that summed up the preoccupations of the time. To defend the château he ordered the digging of the moat that for a long time acted as a barrier in the Cour du Cheval Blanc. He also had the royal apartments doubled in depth, so that from then on they consisted of two enfilades of rooms, one overlooking the Cour Ovale, the other overlooking the Jardin de Diane. Pomp and ceremony had taken off to such an extent in the lifestyle of the last Valois kings[6] that it had become necessary to double the size of the apartment which had amply satisfied the needs of Francis I.

Primaticcio and De l'Orme died in 1570, and Charles IX in 1574, two years after the St. Bartholomew's Day massacre. The reign of Henri III left no trace at Fontainebleau.

The end of the Valois dynasty and the accession of the Bourbons provides a break and allows historians, gasping for breath after the frenetic course of the century, to pause for a moment. However, for the purposes of this book, we have placed the first Bourbon king with the last of the Valois, feeling that the stiletto that killed Henri III made less of a tear in the fabric of history than the one that killed Henri IV. Henri IV did as much for Fontainebleau as Francis I, but he set out "simply to finish the château"[7], to complete it on the same scale and in the same vein, sometimes even the same style. This is self-evident at Fontainebleau, but could it not apply to all aspects of his reign? Henri IV had as good a claim to the throne as

Francis I; both had come from a junior branch of the family and had become king of France without ever having been Dauphin. Henri IV, however, acquired his crown on a battlefield, and his claim to the throne had been contested. He therefore sought out every means to demonstrate the continuity of the monarchy, having had to pick up the thread of history after it had been broken by civil war. The work commissioned by Henri IV at Fontainebleau is exemplary: nothing was destroyed, what was done was integrated into existing work, and what had already been embarked on was finished. If only his descendants had followed his example!

Like Francis I, Henri IV was passionate about building. When he won money playing real tennis (*jeu de paume*) he tended to say, "That will be for my masons". He shared Francis I's fondness for Fontainebleau and like him, and later Louis XIV at Versailles, he enjoyed showing visitors round the château. His concept of what needed doing and how it should be done may explain why the architects working at Fontainebleau during his reign are virtually anonymous, or at any rate not famous. Remy Collin, who drew up the contracts for the Cour des Offices[8] in 1609, has been put forward as the Fontainebleau architect. The name of Jamin who, according to the Abbé Guilbert[9], "excelled in architecture in the reign of Henri IV", has been discounted. Unfortunately Guilbert confused Gracieux Jamin (or Jasmin, Jamyn), the true architect of the Cour des Offices, with his son François Jamin, who was patently too young to have been involved in the undertaking[10]. But Jamin is no more famous than Collin. In other parts of the château, particularly the wing containing the Galerie de Diane which was naturally more elaborate since it was a nobler part of the château, other names must probably be sought. Henri IV was known to refuse to appoint a chief architect who would have been superior to others, and at the Louvre he divided the long wing of the gallery facing the Seine in two, entrusting one half to Jacques II Androuet Du Cerceau and the other to Louis Métezeau. It has been postulated that one or other of these two may have played a role at Fontainebleau, or even Salomon de Brosse, the most famous architect in the early decades of the seventeenth century.

The contribution of Alexandre Francine, the brother of Thomas should also be considered. The Francini (or Francine, Franchine) family originated from Florence, a family of hydraulic engineers or fountain-makers, who were stewards of the royal waters and forests over a period of 160 years. The first family members, the brothers Thomas and Alexandre, arrived in 1598 and were active throughout the first half of the seventeenth century. Thomas created the fountains at Fontainebleau (the Tiber fountain) but it was mainly for the fountains he created at Saint-Germain

Portrait of Henri IV, sixteenth-century French school

Henri IV, who shared Francis I's fondness for Fontainebleau and his love
of building, completed the work started by his predecessor.

Elements of the Belle Cheminée

The Belle Cheminée which gave its name to the wing built by Primaticcio in 1564–1570
was made by the sculptor Matthieu Jacquet dit Grenoble. Commissioned by Henri IV in 1597
and installed in the great hall on the first floor of that wing, it was dismantled in 1725, although
almost all the pieces were preserved. The central relief depicting Henri IV
on horseback originally stood out against a dark background. The two allegorical figures
in the form of statues in the round were *Clemency* and *Peace*. The relief depicting
the *Battle of Ivry* was placed at the centre of the mantlepiece between two Victories. Beside it,
one of the four *putti* bearing the king's cipher, the crown, the Navarre coat of arms
and fleurs-de-lys which were at the top of the side pedestals.

The Belle Cheminée

The section of the wing shown in D'Orbay's 1676 measured drawing gives the composition
of the chimney-piece before it was destroyed.

Galerie des Cerfs

Following pages:
The gallery is named after the stags' heads that decorate it. The walls were painted
by Louis Poisson c. 1600 with bird's eye views of the royal forests and houses, and the ceiling
was decorated with paintings of hunting trophies in 1639 by Louis Poisson's son, Pierre.
The gallery was very much altered in the eighteenth century, and in 1865–1868 it had
to be completely reinstated. It houses several statues, including five of the bronzes made
by Primaticcio after antique models in 1540: the *Laocoön*, the *Cnidian Venus*, the *Apollo Belvedere,*
the *Commodus Hercules* and the *Ariadne of the Vatican.*

that he was famous. He drew inspiration from the Boboli gardens and those created by Pratolino for the Grand-Duke of Tuscany. In 1602 Alexandre was responsible simply for the upkeep of the waters and fountains at Fontainebleau, but he also drew a bird's eye view of the château, engraved by Michel Lasne in 1614, which provides a valuable record of the state of the château at the end of Henri IV's reign. Furthermore, in 1640 he published a collection of doors under the title *Livre d'architecture* which is a monument to Baroque extravagance. Although none of the "auricular" ornaments (ear-shaped, resembling a limp Dali-style watch) he was so fond of are to be found there, the drawings for the gallery may perhaps be attributed to him, more disciplined in style perhaps because they were in some ways subject to state requirements.

While the fountains were the undisputed territory of an Italian family, a family that soon adopted French nationality, the gardens were controlled by the French Mollet family. The presence of Claude Mollet, the most famous member of his family, at Fontainebleau in 1595 is uncontested.

The tradition of French-style sculpture made its first appearance at Fontainebleau with the Belle Cheminée, a chimney-piece that was the masterpiece of Matthieu Jacquet, and that lent its name to the wing built by Primaticcio. Matthieu was the heir of both Germain Pilon and a family of sculptors probably from Grenoble who used the name Jacquet dit Grenoble[11]. In the room approached via the large outside staircase designed by Primaticcio which led to the royal apartments there was an equestrian figure of Henri IV between the figures of Clemency and Peace. This monument which the Bourbons should have venerated was dismantled under the orders of Louis XV.

The painters employed at Fontainebleau illustrate the transition that took place during Henri IV's reign. These painters were either French or Flemish, and constituted the Second School of Fontainebleau. This group still followed the practices of international Mannerism. The work of the most talented among them, Toussaint Dubreuil, who had been trained by Ruggiero de Ruggieri, the last representative of the Italian team, and who also became his son-in-law, ushers in the grand manner of the seventeenth-century French school.

Unfortunately the work of Dubreuil, who was the first of Henri IV's painters, was cut short by his premature death and subsequently has been almost entirely destroyed. There is nothing left of the *Vie d'Hercule* painted with Ruggieri in the Pavillon des Poêles, which was his main work. The paintings in the Galerie des Chevreuils (now destroyed) and the Galerie des Cerfs, which had been attributed to Dubreuil, were in fact by the painter Louis Poisson. A few vestiges of the

Cybele awakening sleep by Toussaint Dubreuil

This picture, still at Fontainebleau, comes from the château of Saint-Germain-en-Laye.
None of the decorations created for Fontainebleau by this eminent representative
of the second School of Fontainebleau has survived.

extensive set of paintings he carried out at Saint-Germain-en-Laye have been brought to Fontainebleau.

The career of artist Martin Fréminet prefigures those of the French classical painters. He trained as a painter in Rome, not at Fontainebleau. On the death of Toussaint Dubreuil in 1602, Henri IV recalled Fréminet and made him his chief painter. Fréminet, who was familiar with the work of Michelangelo, returned the school to the period of Rosso, the keynotes being *terribilità*, drama of colour and tragedy of form. Fréminet's brother-in-law, on the other hand, Ambrosius Bosschaert (or Ambroise Dubois), who was born in Antwerp and appointed Painter to the Queen in 1606, perpetuated the tradition of Primaticcio by a prolific output of work at Fontainebleau.

The school of Fontainebleau

The two schools of Fontainebleau • The Galerie François Premier •
The Galerie d'Ulysse • The Salle de Bal
The three manners of the First School of Fontainebleau • Galerie de Diane,
the story of Clorinda and the story of Theagenes • The Trinité church •
The School of Fontainebleau and international Mannerism.

Two Schools of Fontainebleau have been identified, the first dominated by Italians and active from the 1530s to the 1550s – or even the 1560s, due to the exceptional longevity of Primaticcio who died in 1570 – and the second consisting mainly of French and Flemish artists and coinciding with the reign of Henri IV. The word "school" has a different meaning in each case. The second group did not create a school as such, but attended the school represented by the first; in a way it was no more than an internal echo, the Fontainebleau sector of the international spread of the art of Fontainebleau. It did not teach any lessons, but did bring new life to French painting, which was to shine so brilliantly in the seventeenth century. There was a break between the schools when the Pléiade and the civil war occurred. Strictly speaking, if we simply consider the halt to work at Fontainebleau caused by the Wars of Religion, the political break was in fact quite short, from 1570 to 1580, during the reign of Henri III. But in reality is was longer. Neither Henri II nor Henri IV seems to have been personally involved in making the decisions that would define the school. The Italianate taste of the monarchs, introduced to the Loire Valley by Charles VIII, experienced its second wind under Francis I, whose involvement was considerable. The Italians were well aware of this; they despised the French, but felt admiration and gratitude for the generous monarch ruling over such a nation of barbarians, an enlightened prince who on one of the frescoes in his gallery asks the gods to remove the blindfold from his subjects' eyes.

The decoration that was applied to the château in the sixteenth century was part of the European trend known as Mannerism, but it had peculiarities which

Salle de Bal, measured drawing by Charles Percier, 1793

Detail of a spandrel depicting Apollo and the Muses.

La Galerie François Premier by Alfred Guesdon

The interest of this engraving published in 1837 in *Les Arts au Moyen âge* lies in the fact that it predates the major restoration of the gallery undertaken in 1846. We can see that the composition of the middle of the north wall of the gallery – level with the people – included a chimney-piece, with a large oval motif framed by triple caryatid terms above it. The fireplace was created in 1786, when the width of the gallery wing was doubled and the side-room opening off the gallery to the north was eliminated. The fireplace covered the site of the door leading into that room, which was originally contained within the height of the panelling – like the door open in the foreground of the engraving. The engraving proves that the caryatid terms do not date from the restoration, as has been suggested.

Wainscoting in the Galerie François Premier

The panel bears the salamander, the emblem of Francis I.

Venus, Bacchus and Cupid by Rosso

This picture, initially oval in shape, is either
the original or an early copy of Rosso's
painting which embellished the west end
of the gallery. It is now in the Musée national
d'art et d'histoire in Luxembourg.

The two ends of the Galerie François Premier

The section taken from the measured drawing
made by François D'Orbay in 1676 (below)
is a valuable testimony to the original state
of the east end of the gallery. In the centre
there is a large oval painting, and on either
side of it a door contained within the height
of the wainscoting and a stucco medallion.
    The 1863 measured drawing by R. Pfnor
(left) shows the west end of the gallery after
the nineteenth-century restorations, more or
less as it is now (the upper frieze was created
by the nineteenth-century restorers who raised
the height of the ceiling; it was lowered again
in the 1960s when the gallery was
"unrestored", and the frieze was removed).
    The west end was originally composed
in the same way as the east one: in 1639
the small side doors were replaced by a large
central door leading into the vestibule,
and the oval painting had to go.

Galerie François Premier: The Sacrifice

This panel features a tall priest beside an altar bearing the "F" of Francis
I. It would seem that offerings are being prepared for a sacrifice
to fertility, which should be seen as a reference to the king's birth.
The stuccos on the left-hand edge were remade in the sixteenth-century
style after a door leading on to the grand
staircase was created in 1686.

Galerie François Premier: Ignorance banished

Blindfolded figures are said to represent ignorance.
The man entering the temple on the right is believed to be Francis I.
This has been seen either as a reference to his cultural policies which
sought to remove the blindfold of ignorance from his subjects' eyes, or
to the religious idea of the monarch as the Defender of the Faith.
The male and female stucco satyrs are believed to represent the vices.

Galerie François Premier: The Elephant

Galerie François Premier: The Unity of the State

Since antiquity the elephant has been seen as a symbol of royalty. This one, which bears the letter "F" and the salamander is apparently Francis I himself. It is thought that the stork is a symbol of filial piety, and the bearded old man at the bottom left Rosso.
In the fresco on the left, the rape of Europa by Jupiter in the form of a bull is depicted; in the one on the right, the rape of Philyra by Saturn in the guise of a horse. The frescoes on both sides are believed to represent the bestiality of passion as opposed to royal wisdom.

Francis I, in Roman dress, is carrying a pomegranate in his hand while the kneeling dwarf is presenting another one to him.
The pomegranate made up of many seeds is a symbol of the State, the various components of which are brought together in the person of the king. Francis I is perhaps identified as Caesar, who unified Gaul. At the sides and below, there are three scenes which have not been identified.

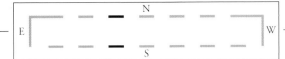

Galerie François Premier: The Fire at Catania

Galerie François Premier: Cleobis and Biton

Two young men save their parents from the fire set off at Catania by the eruption of Mount Etna. This is interpreted as a reference to the sacrifice made by Francis I's two sons who took their father's place in prison in Madrid. On the left and right, two characters usually identified as a Gaul – recognisable from his breeches – and a Roman. This identification is open to dispute, especially the second figure, and we are at a loss to explain its meaning.

Here the twins Cleobis and Biton take the place of oxen killed by the plague and pull the chariot of their mother Cydippe, a priestess of Juno, to the temple. The right-hand medallion depicts the death of the oxen; the left-hand one the twins' eternal sleep, a gift bestowed on them by Juno as a reward for their filial piety. In the stucco panel at the bottom, the Roman figure of Charity can be seen: Pera suckles her imprisoned father, condemned to die of hunger. The whole panel is believed to be a reference to Francis I's love for his mother, Louise of Savoy, who saved the kingdom during the king's captivity in Madrid.

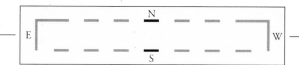

Galerie François Premier: the middle of the gallery

There are problems in reconstructing the successive stages of the middle of the gallery. Our suggestion is that the engraving above by Pierre Milan and
René Boyvin dating from about 1554 should be accepted as Rosso's proposal for the south wall. The *Diana* in the oval, wrongly identified as the
Nymph of Fontainebleau, was to be a stucco figure. As it had not been executed by Rosso, no doubt because he ran out of time,
it was replaced by Primaticcio's *Danaë.* In the small medallions at the top there are the chariots of Diana and her brother Apollo,
shown on the engraving, which obviously accompanied the *Diana* in the oval below. The north wall was adorned with a bust of Francis I framed
by the painted figures of Victory and Renown. This was destroyed at an unknown date. The arrangement we see today was executed
at a later stage after the engraving by Milan and Boyvin: the stucco frame is earlier than 1837. The pseudo-nymph of Fontainebleau was drawn
by Couderc in 1834, and painted in colour by Jean Alaux in 1860.

Galerie François Premier: The Shipwreck

The shipwreck of the Greeks returning from the Siege of Troy was provoked by Nauplius, a Greek who wanted to avenge an affront he had endured during the siege. In the centre, the beacon Nauplius has lit to attract the Greeks. This story may be a reference to the Constable de Bourbon's treachery in transferring his allegiance to Emperor Charles V.

Galerie François Premier: The Death of Adonis

Adonis has been mortally wounded by a wild boar; in her chariot, Venus in tears; on the left, Cybele transformed into a lion. Venus had warned Adonis to be wary of wild animals by telling him the story of the metamorphosis Cybele had carried out in revenge. The whole panel may refer to the accidental death of the young son of Francis I.

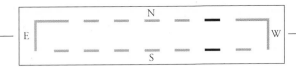

Galerie François Premier: The Education of Achilles

Galerie François Premier: Perpetual Youth

Several of the lessons the centaur Chiron taught to the youthful Achilles are depicted here: swimming, fighting on foot and horseback and, in the background, hunting and music. The theme is the ideal education for a prince, or perhaps also death and immortality, evoked in the fresco on the south wall facing this one. Chiron, who is immortal, has been wounded and implores the gods to allow him to die. Achilles, who has been immersed in the river Styx, can only be wounded on his heel.

The subject is taken from *Theriaca* by Nicander of Colophon, a classical text which Francis I had purchased in manuscript form. Men had been granted perpetual youth by the gods, but did not know how to keep it. The left of the picture depicts the young, the right of it the old, and in the middle sits Youth borne on a donkey. When the donkey wants to drink from the spring guarded by a dragon, the dragon agrees to let him do so on condition that he hands Youth over to him.

Galerie François Premier: Venus thwarted

The fresco is thought to depict Venus trying to wake Cupid
at the request of Hymen, married love, in order to keep back a husband
who is leaving for war. Beneath the fresco a small view depicts
the château of Fontainebleau.

Galerie François Premier: Fight between the Centaurs and the Lapiths

The Centaurs' attack on the Lapiths on the wedding day
of Pirithous and Hippodamia, illustrates the theme of Love disturbed
by war, already illustrated in the fresco opposite.

attracted a following, partly because of Primaticcio's drawings. While there is no explanation for the disappearance of Rosso's drawings for Fontainebleau, there is a reason why so many of Primaticcio's survived. Primaticcio was supplying the needs of a huge workshop, producing only drawings which other artists, such as Nicolò dell'Abate, turned into paintings. This explains why the Fontainebleau style was more or less identified with the style of Primaticcio, who directed work there for almost 40 years.

That said, the main medium through which the ideas of Fontainebleau became famous was not drawing but engraving, and some of the artists in the circle of Rosso and Primaticcio set about engraving the work of the two masters. The design of the Galerie François Premier was reproduced in the form of etchings by the Fontainebleau studio of Antonio Fantuzzi and as engravings by the Paris studio of Pierre Milan and René Boyvin. The intervention of the engravers was not impartial; inevitably they concentrated on motifs that reproduced well in black and white and took liberties with the masters' works.

Disseminating the images by means of tapestry was a more complete but less prolific method. It is already known how widely Raphael's compositions at the Vatican were reproduced using that technique. The *Galerie François Premier tapestries* were made in the château workshops; tradition has it that Francis I commissioned the work with the idea of giving them to Emperor Charles V, but the tapestries were only put on the loom after the famous visit of 1539, perhaps even much later[1]. In any case the intention was certainly to acquaint Europe with the amazing gallery created for the king of France. This objective was achieved, and artists came to Fontainebleau to train. Rubens was the most celebrated "pupil" of the School of Fontainebleau. Theodor van Thulden, himself a follower of Rubens, stayed at Fontainebleau long enough to record the interior decoration, and his engravings provide valuable testimony of works that have been destroyed.

The gallery that bears his name is indeed the work of Francis I. Assisted by a number of humanist scholars, he provided the theme for the scenes depicted by Rosso, a theme that has not been thoroughly unravelled. The gallery is a puzzle, and Francis I was the man who held the key. The room was usually kept locked and the king opened it only to show his guests around it, putting their perspicacity and learning to the test by inviting them to supply their own interpretations. When finally admitting that they were at a loss as they wandered through the labyrinth, the delighted king placed his guests' hands back on the guiding rope. According to one eye-witness, the ambassador Henry Wallop-Calendar, Francis I actually kept the key to the gallery in his pocket[2]. His learned sister Marguerite wrote to her brother: "Your buildings are like a dead body without you [...] Looking at a building without hearing your intentions for it is like reading in Hebrew."[3]

Modern interpreters have tried to unravel this skein of mythological, emblematic and allegorical quotations by re-reading the novels and tales borrowed from classical literature, and by consulting the famous list of emblems drawn up by Andrea Alciati.

Alciati, who taught law in Paris from 1529 to 1534, may have played a part in working out the themes. Almost all the subjects of the twelve main frescoes, six on the north wall and six on the south, have now been explained; it is understood that there was a thematic link between two frescoes facing one another, and the relationship of the subject-matter to the imagery in the frames, where stucco and fresco are combined, has been more or less revealed and understood.

It is still difficult, however, to explain what ties the decoration together. There have been suggestions that involve reading the works from the east of the gallery, or from the west, but no satisfactory conclusion has been reached. The "open sesame" was in the centre. The eastern cycle seems to be philosophical, representing the misfortunes of mankind, and the western cycle political, representing government by the State. The east is believed to be maleficent, and the west beneficent, with the prince acting as a rampart for his subjects against evil. The meaning may seem clear, but Francis I was so ingenious in setting multiple snares and pitfalls along the path of enlightenment that we can never be sure that we have not stumbled upon one of the gallery's blind alleys. Take *L'Incendie*, for example. Two young men are saving their parents from the conflagration set off in Catania by an eruption of Mount Etna. Everything leads to the identification of this fire with the fire at the fall of Troy, and one of the young men with Aeneas bearing his father Anchises to safety. The two fires were associated in ancient texts. Yet once this double reference is worked out, there is still the subject-matter itself. It has been suggested that *L'Incendie* is a reference to the filial devotion of the Dauphin Francis and his brother, Henri, who agreed to be held prisoner in Madrid by Emperor Charles V so that the king could be freed, but this seems too subtle. Moreover, how are the Gaul and Roman figures in stucco framing the scene to be explained?

These themes were turned into images by Rosso and his collaborators between 1535 and 1540. The style is Florentine Mannerism, and there are numerous reminiscences of the *ignudi* painted by Michelangelo on the vaulted ceiling of the Sistine Chapel[4]. If the decoration has no precedent, this is because Michelangelo's heir had to adapt his work to the peculiarities of a French-style gallery, which was long, not very high, and covered with a flat ceiling rather than vaulting. The twelve scenes running along the wall between the ceiling and man-high panelling are reminiscent of the wide-bordered tapestry hangings traditionally used in France to decorate galleries. In the four groups of three frescoes, narrative frames and purely ornamental frames alternate, as do fresco and high-relief frames, so creating triptychs formed by one fresco with a painted border enclosed by two frescoes with relief borders.

The man-high wainscoting is the work of Scibec de Carpi. He was commissioned to make this in ebony and Brazil-wood marquetry, but when it was realised that working in these precious hard woods would take too long, walnut was used for the panelling, which was started in 1539. Scibec also received a commission for a floor and a ceiling, which were either never made or destroyed.

The current gallery is the result of several transformations. In the 1528 specification the wing was to run from the château surrounding the Cour Ovale to the Couvent des Mathurins; but the gallery itself was not to occupy the full length of the wing. At the eastern end, adjoining the bedchamber in the Keep which housed Louise of Savoy, there was to have been a small room, and at the western end a chapel, beside the Couvent des Mathurins. When Francis I moved into the bedchamber in the Keep on his mother's death, when the decoration of the gallery was just starting, the room and the chapel disappeared. The two ends were decorated with an oval painting on canvas by Rosso, depicting Venus and Mars to the east, and Venus, Bacchus and Cupid to the west, contained in a panel framed by two low doors no higher than the wainscoting. Since then the two ends of the room have been radically altered, and the panels destroyed[5]. The drawing Rosso sent to Francis I as evidence of his artistry before coming to France gives some idea of what the *Mars and Venus* in the gallery must have looked like, while the *Venus, Bacchus and Cupid* in the Luxembourg museum may be the original.

Originally the gallery had two small side-rooms to the north and south. The side-room to the north was destroyed in 1786 when the wing was doubled in width along that side. This widening made the windows in the gallery redundant, and they were replaced by false windows during the nineteenth-century restorations. The side-room to the south was doomed as early as the sixteenth century as a result of the construction of a low building along the wing, covered to form a terrace: the room was destroyed in order to make it possible to walk right along the terrace.[(6)] The nineteenth-century restorers altered the original windows on the south wall to create French windows that opened on to the terrace.

The fate of two compositions by Primaticcio depicting the loves of Jupiter has been associated with the fate of the two side-rooms. The *Danaë* which can now be seen in the middle of the south wall of the gallery was painted for the room on the south; and for the north side-room there was a *Semele*, now known only through an engraving. Since the elimination of the rooms also led to the disappearance of the doors leading into the gallery, this apparently created two gaps in the decoration which were filled on the south side by moving the *Danaë*, and on the north by a painting after a sixteenth-century engraving of a figure incorrectly described as a "*Nymphe de Fontainebleau*" – though this did not happen until the nineteenth century. This version of events is unconvincing, for the doors leading into the side-rooms, like those at either end, must have been completely contained within the height of the wainscoting, so that the panelling would only need to have been extended to mask the walled-in doors. In fact there were positions to be filled above the wainscoting in the middle of the north and south walls right from the start. The inscription on the engraving which was used as a model in the nineteenth century identifies the figure as a Diana, not a nymph. It also informs us that it was to be a sculpture – presumably in stucco – and regrets that there had not been enough time for it to be executed. Apparently the composition in question had been intended for the south wall and was partially made; only the oval that had been left empty was later filled – after Rosso's death – using the *Danaë* by Primaticcio, removed from the side-room. The north wall was decorated with a bust of Francis I flanked by the painted figures of Victory and Renown.

It had been accepted that the gallery did not have any fireplaces because there was no obvious way of integrating them into the décor. However, views of the south wall of the wing showed an impressive assortment of chimney stacks. They were Italian-style chimneys, with the hearth and the stack jutting out from the wall so that on the inside there was only a profiled mantelpiece projecting very slightly from the wall, framing the fireplace. There was a chimney on each pier of the south wall, and the drawing of Scibec's wainscoting still perfectly follows the outline of the fireplaces. When doing away with the fireplaces the restorers had to remake the wainscoting on the south wall, copying the wainscoting along the north side where there were no fireplaces[(7)].

Some of the nineteenth-century restorations disappeared when the restoration work was undone in the 1960s. The restorers had thought that the gallery was too low, so they raised the ceiling, which forced them to invent a decorative frieze to run along the top as a link; this was scrapped and the ceiling restored – more or less – to its original height. Bearing all these changes in mind, it is possible to imagine the gallery as it was in Francis I's day: a heated, enclosed space which could only be reached through the bedchamber in the Keep, and had just two modest doors leading out at the other end. It was not designed as a passageway from the château to the monastery (though it may occasionally have been used for that purpose) but rather as the main room of the king's apartments, a covered walkway, a place for reflection; and only its resident lord held its key. The gallery at Fontainebleau was a gallery in the French style, an essential component of an aristocratic residence in France; a beautiful impasse rather than a thoroughfare[8].

The château of Fontainebleau has lost its schoolroom, the Galerie d'Ulysse, in which a great many painters were trained, and which was situated on the first floor of the south range of the Cour du Cheval Blanc. With a length of 150 metres it was probably the longest gallery in Europe. It was not intended as means of circulating, any more than the Galerie François Premier. It was no doubt intended to be a complement to the royal apartments once they had been moved into the wing between the Cour de la Fontaine and the Cour du Cheval Blanc, a move not made until the reign of Henri II. The gallery was decorated with 58 scenes, most of them from *The Odyssey* but a few from *The Iliad*. There was some uncertainty over which of Homer's epic tales to choose, the story of the Trojan War or that of Ulysses's homeward journey. These epics were highly esteemed at the French court, the belief being that the royal family was descended from Francus, the son of Hector the Trojan. The barrel vault was covered with grotesques and mythological scenes, surrounded by a low-relief stucco frame. After the exceptional exuberance of the stucco reliefs in the Galerie François Premier, there was a return here to the technique perfected in Raphael's *Loggie* at the Vatican. According to Abbé Guilbert[9], the vaulting bore the ciphers and emblems of Francis I in some places, and those of Henri II, Charles IX and Henri IV in others. The execution of the decoration from drawings prepared by Primaticcio must have only been started c. 1546, shortly before Francis I's death[10].

The Salle de Bal has survived the ravages of time and the sometimes inopportune zeal of restorers. As early as the reign of Henri IV the frescoes had to be restored. In the reign of Louis-Philippe, Jean Alaux went over them with wax; the wainscoting and the ceiling were almost completely remade and a new floor installed. In the 1960s there was a major restoration (undoing some of the earlier

Decoration of the vaulting of the Galerie d'Ulysse

It took 50 years to paint the 150-metres-long Galerie d'Ulysse, which was destroyed
in 1738–1739. The scheme based on Primaticcio's drawings was started in the final years of
Francis I's reign. From 1559 work on site was supervised by Nicolò dell'Abate,
then by Toussaint Dubreuil in the reign of Henri IV. The walls were covered with 58 scenes from
the *Odyssey*, known through Theodor van Thulden's engravings which were published in 1633.
The vaulting was embellished with grotesques framing mythological scenes.

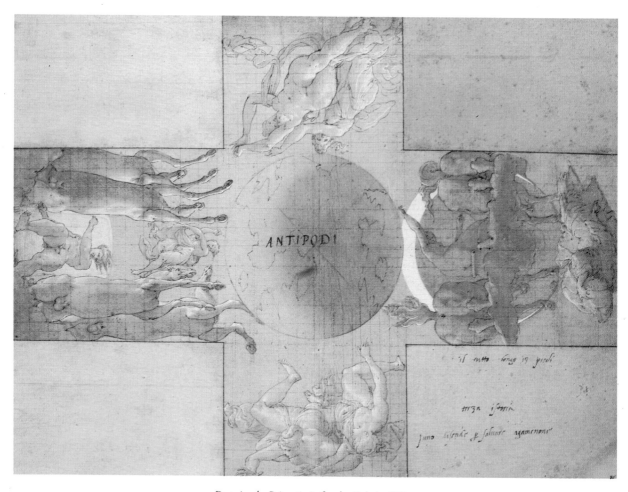

Drawing by Primaticcio for the Galerie d'Ulysse

This preparatory drawing depicts the earth's globe with the chariots of Diana and Apollo.

Salle de Bal, measured drawing
by Rodolphe Pfnor, 1863

Page opposite: *Salle de Bal,*
measured drawing by
Charles Percier, 1793

Drawing by Primaticcio for the Galerie d'Ulysse

This preparatory drawing illustrates the sign of Taurus.

Salle de Bal, measured drawing by Charles Percier, 1793

Le Breton started work on the ballroom in the final years
of Francis I's reign when its ceiling took the form of a tunnel
vault with a basket arch, which has left its mark on the end walls.
The geminate corbels which supported the transverse ribs have also been
preserved. Philibert De l'Orme replaced the vaulting
with a boarded ceiling, with a coffered ceiling suspended from it,
made by Scibec de Carpi in 1550, at the same time as the wainscoting.
The painted decoration was based entirely on Primaticcio's drawings.
The stucco-framed frescoes probably predate the removal
of the vaulting. The spandrels were painted after 1550 by a studio
team supervised by Nicolò dell'Abate. The theme is complex
and obscure; all the gods on Olympus are featured. In 1834
the frescoes were very heavily restored – almost repainted – and
the ceiling, wainscoting and floor were remade.
In 1963 some of the repainted work was removed;
the wainscoting was recarved using a remnant of
the sixteenth-century panelling as a model.

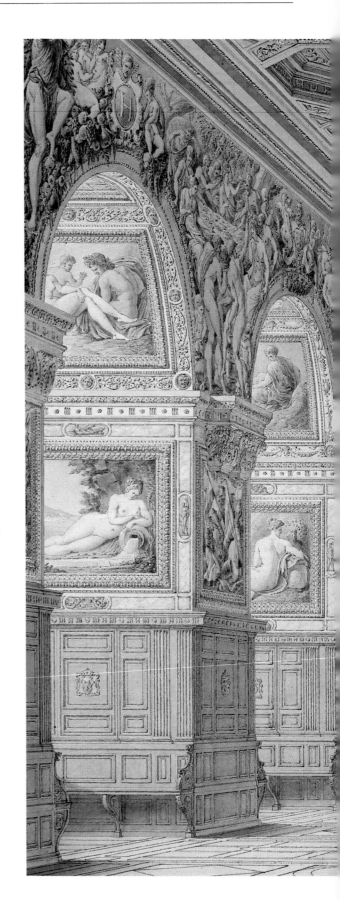

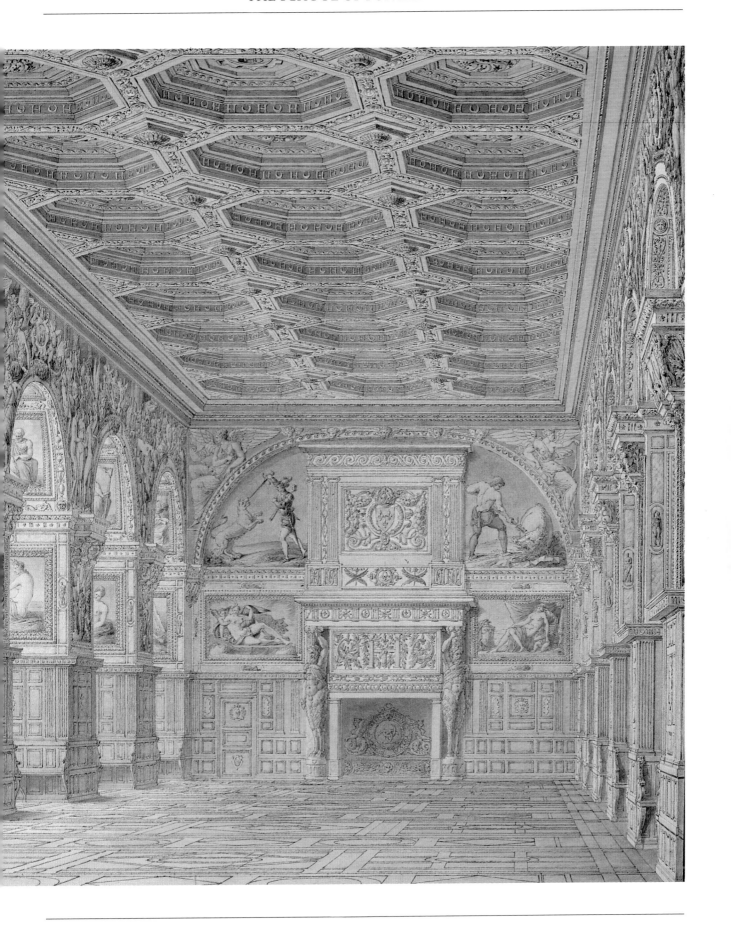

restoration): some of Alaux's work had to be spared to avoid creating gaps, and the nineteenth-century wainscoting was recarved based on sixteenth-century guidelines. However, the causes behind the deterioration were not successfully eradicated, and are once again taking their toll.

The Salle de Bal wing was one of the parts built by Le Breton and repaired by De l'Orme. In the actual Salle de Bal, De l'Orme replaced the barrel vaulting with a boarded ceiling, and a coffered ceiling below. Decisions were made quickly: three months after being commissioned by the king, De l'Orme completed a contract on 13 July 1548 for the construction of two wooden floors, one to bear the room and the other to cover it (by floor we mean here a horizontal structure consisting of beams and joists, not to be confused with either the ceiling or the actual flooring). On 19 February and 4 June 1550 Scibec signed contracts to make the flooring, the wainscoting, the joinery work for the windows, benches in the window embrasures, and the coffered ceiling – the first of its kind to be made in France – all following De l'Orme's drawings[11]. The decorative work must have been well advanced in 1556 since De l'Orme had the chimney-piece painted and gilded that year.

Based on this information the fresco and stucco decoration was carried out between 1550 and 1556. However, a distinction should perhaps be made between the stucco decoration that covers the window recesses and the walls between the top of the wainscoting and the cornices, and the decoration that continues on the spandrels. There is no question that the whole scheme is the work of Primaticcio; his drawings for both areas have been preserved. But the first type of decoration almost certainly dates back to the final years of Francis I's reign, which would make it contemporary with the first decorative work in the Galerie d'Ulysse, which uses the same approach. In fact Le Breton's vaulting was not only intended, it was actually built. If this had not been the case, there is surely no reason for the composition of the two end walls of the room to have been designed to fit under the top of a basket arch. Likewise the fact that the corbels supporting the transverse ribs of the vaulting were not removed once they ceased to have a purpose was because the decoration below them had already been carried out, and a new start would have been necessary if the corbels were removed. In other words it is our belief that the first part of the decoration was carried out while the vaulted roof was in place, and it is only the spandrels that should be dated to the period 1550–1556. Only that area could have been executed by the workshop of Nicolò dell'Abate who did not arrive in France until 1552.

There were three successive decorative manners at Fontainebleau during the time of the Italians: the one used in the Galerie François Premier, the one in the Galerie d'Ulysse and the lower parts of the Salle de Bal, and the one in the upper parts of the

First Galerie de Diane, measured drawing by Charles Percier, 1793

The Galerie de Diane wing, or the queen's wing, was built in the reign of Henri IV.
The Galerie de Diane on the first floor formed part of the queen's apartment.

Salle de Bal. A comparison between the Galerie François Premier and the Salle de Bal powerfully demonstrates the uniqueness of the former, a royal *tour de force* that defied reproduction. For this reason artists took a greater interest in the Galerie d'Ulysse and the Salle de Bal. According to the bookseller and engraver Pierre-Jean Mariette, "Poussin said that he knew of nothing more suitable than the sequence of great subjects in the Galerie d'Ulysse to train a painter and fire his genius"[12]. Abbé Guilbert wrote of the Galerie d'Ulysse: "The great masters came to study the drawings and used the originals as a training"[13]. Charles Percier, who later collaborated with Pierre-François Fontaine on the buildings of the Empire and Restoration periods, stopped at Fontainebleau on his way back from Rome, his mind still "filled with memories of Italy". The "strangeness" of the château complex amazed him. He enjoyed discovering the works of the Italians, but it was only in the Salle de Bal that he had the impression of really being back in Italy. As a result, he made a detailed drawing in 1793, a valuable work since it predates the nineteenth-century restorations[14].

By great good fortune Percier went to Fontainebleau before Napoleon ordered the destruction of the Galerie de Diane, the main achievement of Ambroise Dubois (created c. 1601–1606?), a few remnants of which can be found in the château. Percier's measured drawing[15] revealing details of the decoration of this gallery, still

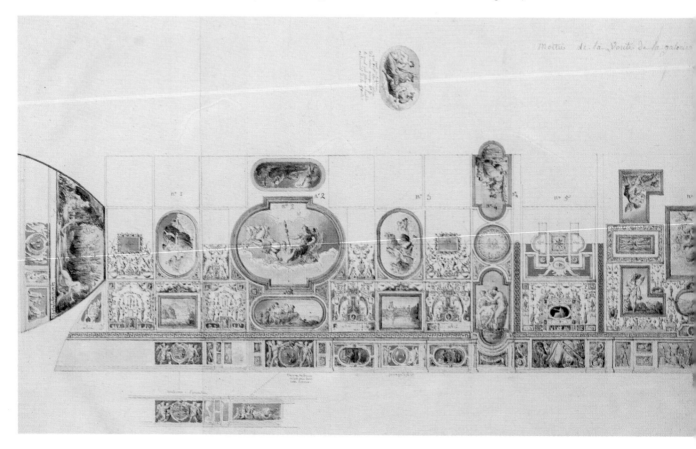

known at the time as the Galerie de la Reine because it was part of the queen's apartment. It did not lead anywhere. The story of Diana occupied only the first third of the gallery, while the last third told the story of Diana's brother, Apollo. The central part with portraits of Henri IV and Marie de' Medici and ten panels depicting the king's victories was not the work of Dubois, but was by another artist whose name is not known.

The few pictures preserved in the Cabinet de Clorinde, a small room also attached to the queen's apartment, are further remnants of Dubois's work. In this small room Dubois had painted the story of Tancredes and Clorinda taken from Tasso's *Jerusalem Delivered*. No doubt it was this work that earned Dubois the title

First Galerie de Diane, measured drawing by Charles Percier, 1793

This gallery had been decorated by Ambroise Dubois c. 1601–1606 with paintings based on themes from the story of Diana and that of Apollo. The central part, depicting Henri IV, Marie de' Medici and the king's victories, was by an unknown artist. The whole of this decorative scheme disappeared at the beginning of the nineteenth century.

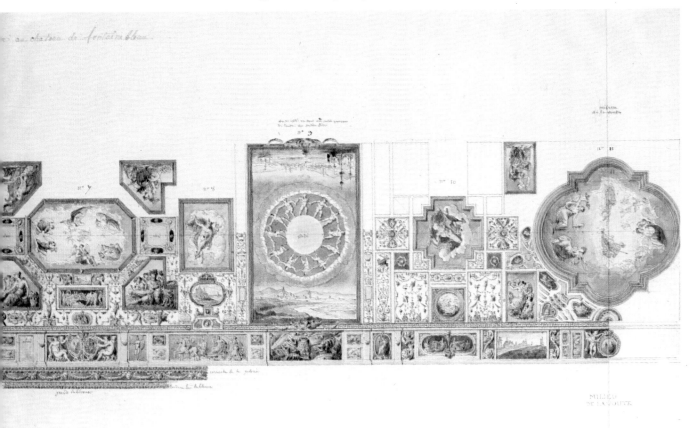

Story of Tancred and Clorinda: "The Meeting of Tancred and Clorinda"
and *'"The Fight between Tancred and Clorinda outside Jerusalem"* by Ambroise Dubois

This story, taken from Tasso's *Jerusalem Delivered*, was illustrated through eight scenes
which embellished a room known as the Cabinet de Clorinde attached to the queen's apartment,
with windows overlooking the Jardin de Diane. The room was destroyed in 1747.

The Story of Theagenes and Chariclea: "'The Abduction of Chariclea by Theagenes"
and *"The Abduction of Chariclea by Trachin"* by Ambroise Dubois

The pictures from *Aethiopica* (the story of Theagenes and Chariclea), a fourth-century Greek
romance translated in the sixteenth century by Amyot, were painted by Ambroise Dubois from
1605 onward for the Cabinet Ovale, known as the Salon Louis XIII.

Trinité church

The building of the church was started at the end of Francis I's reign and finished
by Philibert De l'Orme in the reign of Henri II. Nothing remains of the first decorative scheme
carried out in 1554 by Scibec de Carpi from De l'Orme's drawings. The present decoration
is the work of Martin Fréminet who started on the vaulting in 1608. The engraving depicting
the marriage by proxy of King Charles II of Spain to Marie-Louise of Orleans shows the way
the iron balconies were used during ceremonies. At that time the oval medallions between
the windows were decorated with paintings by Martin Fréminet – not completed –
which were replaced in the eighteenth century.

Vaulting of the Trinité church

Martin Fréminet was summoned by Henri IV after spending 25 years in Italy, and was entrusted
with large-scale religious painting. He devised the iconographic programme
for the church and provided drawings both for the religious subjects and the ornamental parts.

Scheme for the high altar of the Trinité church by Martin Fréminet

The present high altar was made in 1628 by the sculptor Francesco Bordoni,
after a noticeably different drawing by Fréminet (died 1619).

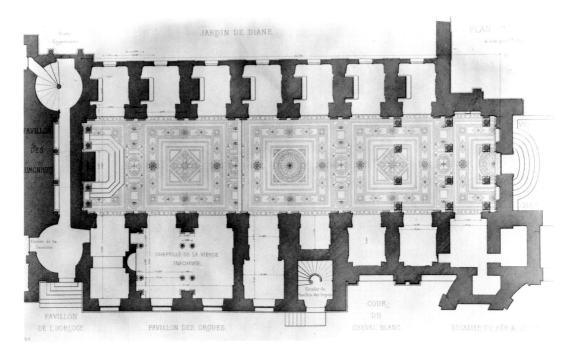

Plan of the Trinité church, measured drawing by Rodolphe Pfnor, 1863

This plan enables us to see the columns of three arches on the left, behind the choir,
in a corridor that forms part of the Pavillon des Armes; these are probably the remains
of the Mathurins' cloister, built in 1528. At the bottom, the Chapelle de la Vierge,
formerly the Mathurins' choir, which was created in 1664 by combining and widening
two earlier chapels, and the staircase of the Pavillon des Orgues.

Elevation of the Trinité church, measured drawing by Rodolphe Pfnor, 1863

The state of the chapel in 1863 is different both from its original and present state. The oval pictures on the piers
dating from the eighteenth century were removed in 1824–1830, and reinstated in 1930. The same
is true of the two large iron balconies running below the windows, which were reinstated in 1978.

of Painter to the Queen in 1606. The cycle of the loves of Theagenes and Chariclea which Dubois painted in the Cabinet Ovale is almost intact. The decoration bears the date of its completion, 1610, which means it dates entirely from Henri IV's reign. While the painter pays his dues to his great Italian predecessors, his approach is typical of French art at the beginning of the seventeenth century: a high wainscoting incorporating painted areas, landscapes, flowers and emblems; large framed paintings; relatively low painted ceilings, and chimney-breasts projecting from the wall.

The vaulted ceiling of the Trinité church painted by Martin Fréminet from 1608, and probably unfinished when the artist died in 1619, is the main locally produced work of the Second School of Fontainebleau, providing a perceptible return to the roots of the school, and the art of Rosso and even Michelangelo. It is easy to see reminiscences in the *La Chute des Anges* of *The Last Judgement* in the Sistine Chapel. This large painted vault is exceptional in itself, and still Italian in genre; fine vaulted stonework in French churches tended to be left unpainted. The theme, provided by the Jesuit, Father Richeôme, is man's Redemption, thus breaking with the tradition of iconography in a church being dependent on its dedication, in this case to the Trinity, because of the Trinitarian monastery.

The decoration of the walls has been reworked several times. New paintings were introduced in the eighteenth century, and there was a variety of restoration work in the nineteenth and twentieth centuries. The decoration carried out by De l'Orme in the reign of Henri II (a choir screen and chapel screens) may already have been sacrificed by the time of Henri IV. Due to lack of time, part of the walls had probably been left unpainted, which would explain the reputed reaction of the Spanish ambassador when Henri IV showed him the new decoration of the royal apartments: "All that is lacking is to provide God with an abode that matches Your Majesty's."

The School of Fontainebleau is a manifestation of the international style of Mannerism which had come from Michelangelo and his followers, including the Tuscans Pontormo and Rosso, and the Emilians Parmigianino and Primaticcio, and was characterised by strident colours, violent gestures, contorted and elongated human bodies, and a systematic use of the nude figure. The school was responsible for popularising in French art images of Venus and Diana that were

Women bathing, engraving by Jean Mignon, after Luca Penni, c. 1547–1550

Luca Penni was one of Rosso's collaborators on the Galerie François Premier. The engraving
is a perfect illustration of the Fontainebleau ideal of female beauty.

distinguished by the beauty of their milky skin and long bodies; art lovers
preferred them as bathing figures. Erudition was exploited to the point of
becoming esoteric. The sagas, taken from mythology in the case of the first school,
and from romances in the case of the second, extended the full length of galleries.
Grotesques mixed figures and ornamental features indiscriminately. In fact it was
in its use of ornamentation that the lesson of Fontainebleau was best understood:
the leather motifs in the Galerie François Premier (shredded, coiled thongs)
appeared on the flat surfaces of book bindings, the frames of frontispieces and
tapestry borders.

From Louis XIII to Louis XVI. And From Napoleon I to Napoleon III

Louis XIII and Anne of Austria • Louis XIV • Louis XV • Louis XVI
Napoleon I • From the Restoration to the present day

The monumental history of the château, a story of continuous embellishment, ended with Henri IV. After him the sovereigns removed as much as they added, a futile operation which evoked as much disapproval as admiration.

Louis XIII had little inclination for the arts and architecture, so progress in his reign was modest. Jean Androuet Du Cerceau, the nephew of Jacques II, remade the horseshoe-shaped flight of steps, but that was because the one constructed by De l'Orme looked likely to collapse. The vestibule which the steps led up to was still waiting to be decorated; the decoration it was given was noteworthy for the fine door leaves carved by Jean Gobert (1639). The king's bedchamber overlooking the Jardin de Diane has retained most of its Louis XIII decoration, and is the fourth bedchamber in the history of the château (after Francis I's bedchamber which became Queen Eleanor's, the bedchamber in the Keep, and the bedchamber in the Pavillon des Poêles). Louis XIII did not instigate this new layout. As already explained, the depth of the wing housing the royal apartments had been doubled in the reign of Charles IX, and the apartments themselves were consequently twice as large. Henri III was probably the first king to abandon the bedchamber in the keep for the new room overlooking the Jardin de Diane. For the same reasons, the queen's bedchamber was moved from the court side to the garden side. Its ceiling, featuring the cipher of Anne of Austria, Louis XIII's widow and the Regent, was made by the joiner Guillaume Noyers in 1644.

Door of the Vestibule du Fer à Cheval

It was Philibert De l'Orme in the mid-sixteenth century who first thought of moving the château's main entrance away from the Porte Dorée to a vestibule created in the middle of the range at the back of the Cour du Cheval Blanc. The idea did not become a reality until the beginning of the seventeenth century. The leaves of three doors were carved by Jean Gobert in 1639.

*King's bedchamber overlooking
the Jardin de Diane,
today the Salle du Trône*

This bedroom, created at the end
of the sixteenth century,
has a decoration that dates mainly
from the end of Louis XIII's reign.
The ceiling bears the king's
coat of arms and his motto
"*Erit haec quoque cognita monstris*"
(even the monsters will know it).

King's bedchamber overlooking the Jardin de Diane,
today the Salle du Trône

On the leaves of the door there are trophies,
a motif inspired from Roman iconography
and intended to glorify King Louis XIII.

King's bedchamber overlooking the Jardin de Diane,
today the Salle du Trône

The piers were added by Jacques Verberckt in 1752–1753.

King's bedchamber overlooking the Jardin de Diane,
today the Salle du Trône

The ceiling with the coats of arms of France
and Navarre date from the reign of Louis XIII.

Queen's bedchamber overlooking the Jardin de Diane, now the Chambre de l'Impératrice

The ceiling was made in 1644, the year following the death of Louis XIII,
for his widow, Anne of Austria.

*Overdoor of the queen-mothers'
bedchamber*

As an overdoor, this is a portrait
of Anne of Austria who had
the queen-mothers' apartment
redecorated in the
mid-seventeenth century.

Ceiling of the queen-mothers' bedchamber

The ceiling of the bedroom redecorated for Anne of Austria by Jean Cotelle.

As Louis XIV neared his majority in 1651, Anne of Austria arranged for the queen-mothers' apartment to be refurbished. It had been occupied by Catherine and, before her, Marie de' Medici, and Anne took up residence there on the king's marriage (1660). The apartment consisted of a suite of rooms – a guards' room, an antechamber, a bedchamber and a study – which occupied the whole first floor of the wing and the Pavillon des Poêles. Little is left of the guards' room which was decorated by Charles Errard in 1662 and 1664. The ceiling, originally intended for the bedchamber of Henri II in the Pavillon des Poêles, was installed in the antechamber in 1659. The bedchamber and the study (no longer in existence) were decorated by Jean Cotelle, a painter and famous ornamental designer. His style is particularly recognisable in the decoration of the wainscoting, but the ceiling, a masterpiece in its own right, is far more powerful. Not much is known of

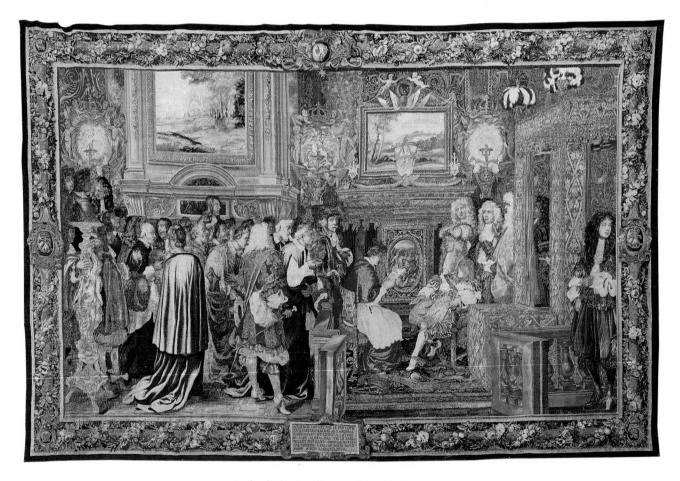

Cardinal Chigi's audience with Louis XIV in 1664

The series of tapestries known as the *Histoire du roi* was woven at the Gobelins from cartoons by Charles Le Brun. The tapestry featuring Cardinal Chigi's audience is preserved at Versailles. The depiction of the king's bedchamber at Fontainebleau where the audience took place is on the fanciful side.

what was destroyed to make way for the new decoration. According to Sauval, a historian from Paris, the prudish Anne of Austria had many pictures from the "immodest" Renaissance destroyed. And as Abbé Guilbert writes: "However much may have been spent [by Anne of Austria in decorating the queen-mothers' apartment], nothing can make us forget the fine wainscoting and ceiling with which Henri II had adorned it"[1]. Henri II's small study built above the Galerie Basse was left untouched, and it completed the queen-mothers' apartment – Abbé Guilbert describes it admiringly. It was not destroyed until the eighteenth century, at the same time as the Pavillon des Poêles.

As he was busy with Versailles, Louis XIV did very little at Fontainebleau, providing only lodgings for the princes, the Secretaries of State, and the officers of the Crown on the Cour des Princes, the Cour des Mathurins and the Jardin des Pins. Despite being designed by the greatest architects in the kingdom, François D'Orbay and Jules Hardouin-Mansart, these buildings were modest in appearance, perhaps because of the issue of hierarchy, but also out of respect for what had gone before. The wainscoting in the apartment of Madame de Maintenon, the only example of Louis XIV style in the interior decoration, has also been effaced, just as the woman herself was expunged from memory.

The images of the reign have failed to illustrate the main event which took place in the château, that is the signature of the second Edict of Fontainebleau, corresponding to that signed by Francis I. On 18 October 1685 the Edict of Nantes, the cornerstone of Henri IV's entire policy for securing religious peace, was revoked, yet the Fontainebleau event that was featured in the famous *Histoire du roi* tapestries, woven at the Gobelins after drawings by Le Brun, was of the audience accorded to Cardinal Chigi by Louis XIV on 29 July 1664 when he came to offer the Pope's apologies because his Corsican guards had molested servants at the French embassy!

Louis XV was the worst of the vandalising kings. It would be tedious to catalogue every example of destruction that he ordered at Fontainebleau, but two are worth noting for the indignation they aroused in his contemporaries. When the Belle Cheminée was dismantled in 1725 so that the room could be turned into a theatre, Abbé Guilbert wrote: "In a matter of hours a monument to the valour and glory of Henry the Great was destroyed; its sole crime being that it was admired as the fruit of five years' labour by Jacquet dit Grenoble, a famous sculptor who had created a masterpiece that deserved to be favoured [over the] shallow beauties

Stag at bay at the Franchard rocks
by Jean-Baptiste Oudry

Like many others, this hunt led by
Louis XV and painted in 1738 ended
at the Franchard rocks, a site that is
particularly typical of the Fontainebleau
landscape. The painter has included
himself in the bottom right-hand
corner of the picture.

of a vile theatre, all too often the rock on which chastity and innocence founder."[2]
The abbé overlooked the fact that Henri IV, the "Vert Galant", was no paragon of
virtue, for all that he was flanked by the figures of Clemency and Peace! Moreover,
even before it was turned into a theatre, performances were given in the room
during the lifetime of Henri IV, for example the ballet *Les Preneurs d'amours*
performed in 1608, which must certainly have been less edifying than *Le Devin de
village*, with words and music by Jean-Jacques Rousseau, which had its première in
Louis XV's theatre on 18 October 1752 – a trifle from the pen of a philosopher
who denounced the immorality of the theatre in his works. It is interesting to read
the passage in *Les Confessions* where Rousseau describes his feelings on hearing
from his box the whispers of women "beautiful as angels" saying quietly to one

another: "This is charming, quite delightful, there isn't a sound that doesn't go straight to the heart"[3]. The abbé knew what he was talking about!

Despite this, Abbé Guilbert was no prude and spoke up in defence of the Galerie d'Ulysse, in which amorous scenes provided a permanent spectacle, when it was being destroyed. "Oh! If only the opinion of connoisseurs and the esteem of the greatest masters who are proud to have made copies of these pictures could have some influence on lovers of novelty!"[4] Count Francesco Algarotti, an authority in matters of taste, witnessed the destruction:

> *I saw once more at Fontainebleau the admirable paintings by our*
> *Nicolino [Nicolò dell'Abate], they still had the freshness, the relief*

Salle du Conseil

The wainscoting and the door panels were adorned with allegories of the Elements, Seasons, Arts, Virtues, etc., treated in *camaïeu* by Carle Van Loo and Jean-Baptiste Pierre. The flowers and trophies are by Alexis Peyrotte. The ceiling is decorated with five paintings by François Boucher.

and the powerful colouring they had when Vasari described them. The adventures of Ulysses as recounted by Homer were the subject of these paintings composed by Primaticcio and executed by Nicolò. I cannot express the pleasure I felt in admiring this poetry in images. However, if I had delayed just a few hours, it would have been too late, and I would have had to regret the loss for ever. The masons were already on the roof of the gallery which they were demolishing; débris from the vaulted roof of this monument was falling on our heads, and we had to beg the

Door of the Salle du Conseil

Autumn is depicted on the left leaf, winter on the right.

Ceiling of the Salle du Conseil

Ceiling by François Boucher depicting the sun driving night away.

workmen to suspend their devastation for a moment to give ourselves time to contemplate the faithful dog which recognises and fawns upon his old master, and to see Ulysses stretching his powerful bow and defying the effeminate pretenders to Penelope's hand.[5]

In 1759 Mariette, an authority, expressed regret: "The paintings on the vaulted ceiling were no small treasure, and it is impossible to deplore their destruction adequately. When the decision was taken, they were as fresh and bright as they had ever been."[6] Ulysses's dog must be overlooked, however, in order to admire the hounds that Louis XV set loose amongst the rocks of the forest of Fontainebleau to track down deer, painted by Jean-Baptiste Oudry in some hunting scenes.

Whatever the merits of the Gros Pavillon (1750–1754) and the Louis XV wing (1739–1740 for the east end, 1773–1774 for the west end), it is impossible

Door of the Salle du Conseil

On the bottom of this door there is an allegorical representation of Earth.

to forget that they replaced the Pavillon des Poêles and the wing containing the Galerie d'Ulysse, areas sacrificed for a grand design that was never completed. The plan was to rebuild the Cour du Cheval Blanc in its entirety: Jacques Gabriel and his son Jacques-Ange Gabriel did not even manage to rebuild the wing that was destroyed along its length, and were two bays short of reaching the corner pavilion, which was spared along with the Grotte des Pins concealed in its base wall.

The Salle du Conseil (1751–1753) with its *camaïeu* work by Carle Van Loo and Jean-Baptiste Pierre excites admiration, but when you look up at the ceiling paintings by François Boucher you recognise the characteristic construction of a ceiling dating from the first half of the seventeenth century – adjoining rooms, the Cabinet Ovale and the bedchamber of Louis XIII, still have their decoration intact. In the reign of Henri IV the Salle du Conseil was the king's study, and according to Abbé Guilbert the wainscoting was "delicately charged and richly embellished by several paintings and *camaïeu* figures". Louis XV at least preserved the *camaïeu* technique![7]

Some exceptional works were introduced to the interior in Louis XVI's reign, and they can be appreciated all the more because nothing was mutilated

Scheme for the queen's apartment by Pierre-Marie Rousseau

The architect Pierre-Marie Rousseau left several schemes
– including this one, dated 1786 – which probably related to a complete redecoration
of the queen's apartment.

to make way for them. In 1777 Richard Mique, Queen Marie-Antoinette's architect who had created the Trianon *hameau* at Versailles, started decorating the Turkish boudoir on the second floor, above the queen's apartment. In 1786 the architect Pierre Rousseau embellished the apartment with two masterpieces of French decorative art: the Salon des Jeux and the boudoir. Two years previously Rousseau had doubled the depth of the wing containing the Galerie François Premier, adding a suite of rooms overlooking the Jardin de Diane.

At Versailles Louis XVI had given orders for Gabriel's grand design to enclose the courtyard side of Louis XIV's château to be carried out and it is thought that, to escape the disruption caused by this work, Louis XVI acquired the château of Rambouillet and had the wing at Fontainebleau doubled in depth. However, it was late in the day to embark on such a venture.

The Revolution resulted in Primaticcio's bronzes being taken to the Musée des Arts, although they have since been returned to Fontainebleau. Furnishings were also dispersed; through auctions the Musée National du Château de Fontainebleau

Salon des jeux de la Reine, or Grand Salon de l'Impératrice

These grotesques were painted by Michel-Hubert Bourgois and Jacques-Louis-François Touzé
from drawings by the architect Pierre-Marie Rousseau. Rousseau was inspired by Piranesi, whom
he may have met in Rome when he was there on an allowance from the king.

Salon des jeux de la Reine,
or Grand Salon de l'Impératrice

This room which was part
of the queen's apartment,
overlooking the Jardin de Diane,
has a 1786 decoration, inspired by the antique
style and Raphael's Loggie at the Vatican.
The overdoors are *trompe-l'oeil* images
by Piat-Joseph Sauvage, a specialist
in that genre, accompanied by plaster
sphinxes made by the sculptor
Philippe-Laurent Roland.
The ceiling is embellished with
an image of Minerva crowning the Muses
by the painter Jean-Simon Barthélemy.

The decoration of this room
in the queen's apartment
overlooking the Jardin de Diane
is a masterpiece of decorative art.
It was carried out by the same artists
and in the same style as the Salon des Jeux
de la Reine: designed by the architect
Pierre-Marie Rousseau; the grotesques
painted by Michel-Hubert Bourgois
and Jacques-Louis-François Touzé; the
ceiling depicting Aurora by Barthélemy;
the overdoor depicting the Muses
by Philippe-Laurent Roland; the bronzes
in the chimney-piece and
the espagnolettes by Pitoin.

Overdoor of the Boudoir de la Reine

Euterpes, the Muse of lyric poetry, and Terpsichore, the Muse of dance,
both high reliefs by Philippe-Laurent Roland.

Decoration of the Boudoir de la Reine

On the left, an espagnolette by Pitoin; on the right, a panel of the wainscoting.

Second Galerie de Diane by Thomas Allom, water-colour, 1839

This was started in 1810 by the architect Maximilien-Joseph Hurtault who was inspired by the Grande Galerie at the Louvre. Work stopped with Napoleon's abdication in 1814, by which point the ornamental decoration was complete, and resumed in 1817. The iconographic programme chosen by Napoleon was then abandoned, and in 1822–1825 the vaulting was painted by Mery-Joseph Blondel and Alexandre Abel de Pujol with the story of Diana. The walls were covered by sixteen pictures of the history of the monarchy. In 1858 Napoleon III moved the château's library to the gallery, which led to the pictures being removed and the set broken up in 1875.

has acquired some items. Most of the pieces that can be seen there today are the result of the refurnishing programme undertaken by Napoleon I.

Napoleon destroyed the Galerie de Diane because it was in ruins; the wing closing off the Cour du Cheval Blanc was destroyed because he preferred open courtyards to closed ones. However, his architect Maximilien-Joseph Hurtault did one positive thing by starting the new Galerie de Diane. When finished it would be regarded as one of the outstanding examples of decorative art in the first half of the nineteenth century. Hurtault also designed the Jardin Anglais in 1810–1812 in place of the Jardin des Pins, and in 1803 the Manège or riding school, used by the military school set up at Fontainebleau by Bonaparte. The school occupied part of the château until it again became the sovereign's residence. Napoleon had a sense of history, which inspired him with respect for the château, described by him as a "house of the centuries". He set about placing it on the historical map.

Galerie de Diane

The gallery which had been decorated in the first half of the nineteenth century
was turned into a library by Napoleon III, and the paintings depicting key moments in the history
of the monarchy which decorated the walls were removed at the same time.

Napoleon by François Girard

This portrait of Napoleon painted in 1805 shows him wearing the coronation robes
designed by the painter Isabey.

On 25 November 1804 Pope Pius VII (who had signed the Concordat with Bonaparte in 1801) was received at Fontainebleau and on 2 December he made the general an emperor. On 19 June 1812 he was back at Fontainebleau, but this time as a prisoner. On 25 January 1813, under duress, he signed the second concordat, the Concordat of Fontainebleau, which was in favour of Gallic propositions. The Pope's reaction when subjected first to Napoleon's cajoling, then to his threats, is well known: *"Commediànte! Tragediànte!"* The tragedy was drawing to a close. Abandoning a scheme to make Paris the papal seat, Napoleon freed Pius VII on 23 January 1814; his confinement at Fontainebleau lasted nineteen months. Such hospitality deserved to be repaid. A few years later Pius VII granted the Bonaparte family asylum in his territory.

In April 1814, two months after the Pope returned to Rome, Napoleon abdicated. In the preceding days Paris, which had not seen a foreign army for four centuries since the worst periods of the Hundred Years' War, opened its gates to the Allies. Napoleon's abdication document contains these words:

> *The allied powers having proclaimed that the Emperor Napoleon was*
> *the sole obstacle to the re-establishment of peace in Europe, Emperor*
> *Napoleon, loyal to his oath, declares that on his own behalf and on*
> *behalf of his heirs he renounces his claim to the throne of France and*
> *Italy because there is no personal sacrifice, including the sacrifice of his*
> *life, that he is not ready to make in the interest of the French people.*

In his *Mémoires d'Outre-Tombe* Chateaubriand comments: "The emperor did not take long to provide, with his return, an emotional repudiation of these words: he needed only long enough to go the island of Elba." On 20 April 1814 the famous farewell scene – *Les Adieux de Napoléon à la garde impériale dans la cour du Cheval blanc* – took place in the Cour du Cheval Blanc. To quote Chateaubriand:

> *Napoleon came down the double flight of steps leading to the*
> *peristyle of the deserted palace of the Capetian monarchy. A few*
> *grenadiers, the remnants of the soldiers who had conquered Europe,*
> *lined up in the large courtyard, as if on their last battlefield.*

Manège, Boulevard du Maréchal-Juin

This was built in 1807 by the architect Maximilien-Joseph Hurtault for the École militaire founded at Fontainebleau by Napoleon in 1803. The wooden frame consists only of small planks assembled together, following the technique used by De l'Orme.

Napoleon's farewell to the Imperial Guard in the Cour du Cheval Blanc
by Antoine Montfort, after Horace Vernet

Napoleon abdicated on 6 April 1814, and on 20 April he took leave
of the Guard before embarking for the island of Elba.

Interview between Napoleon I and Pius VII on 26 November 1804
by Jean-Louis Demarne and Alexandre Dunouy

This 1808 picture commemorates the Pope's visit to France for the coronation
of the emperor which took place on 2 December 1804.

Bonaparte addressed these words to the last witnesses of his battles:
"Generals, officers, warrant officers and soldiers of my old guard,
I bid you farewell: for twenty years I have been pleased with you,
and have always found you on the path of glory."

The restored monarchy commissioned the painters Mery-Joseph Blondel and Abel de Pujol to complete the decoration of the new Galerie de Diane, dedicated to the myth of the chaste huntress goddess, while the walls were adorned with pages from the history of France. Napoleon III removed these, not as an act of censorship, but replacing them with shelving for the château's library. What little there is to say about Napoleon III is favourable. He enhanced the Louis XV wing by adding a theatre designed by the architect Hector Lefuel (1854) and enriched the Gros Pavillon with Chinese-style drawing-rooms.

During Louis-Philippe's reign the idea of a national museum at Fontainebleau was first considered (as it was simultaneously at Versailles). It is hard to judge the project. On the one hand, it ensured the preservation of the paintings in the Galerie François Premier and the Salle de Bal, but it also allowed the hotchpotch of the chimney-piece in the Salle des Gardes, where elements of the Belle Cheminée, which had been dismantled, were stuck on to the remains of the chimney-piece from the bedchamber of Henri II. Twentieth-century restorers have not dared to undo the deed, and they were right to leave it.

The loss of irreplaceable works by Rosso and Primaticcio (including paintings in the Appartement des Bains, the Pavillon des Poêles and the Pavillon de Pomone) is so great that it is easy to forget that Fontainebleau was one of the most

Stained glass in the lower Saint-Saturnin chapel

Made at Sèvres in 1834–1836 after drawings by Marie of Orleans,
the daughter of King Louis-Philippe.

*Wedding cabinet of Duke Ferdinand of Orléans and Princess Helen
of Mecklenburg-Schwerin in 1837*

Porcelain plaques depict the civil marriage in the Salle de Bal,
the Catholic ceremony in the Trinité church, and the Protestant ceremony
in the Salle des Colonnes, beneath the Salle de Bal.

Theatre

This was built by Hector Lefuel in 1854 in the Louis XV wing.

imposing châteaux of the French Renaissance. The Musée National du Château de Fontainebleau is dedicated to displaying Empire furnishings, and its collection is incomparable. But is this the proper vocation for a château where the Bonapartes counted for so little? Fortunately a few *Ancien régime* pieces have come to Fontainebleau, including the mid-seventeenth century ebony cabinet reproducing the scenes in the Galerie d'Ulysse after Van Thulden's engravings, the superb Boulle clock (c. 1725), and works by cabinet-makers such as Beneman, Riesener, Sené and Jacob. Although Georges Jacob, who was imprisoned during the Terror, did not lose his head in the Revolution, he may perhaps have lost his touch: the works produced by the Jacob-Desmalter firm for Napoleon are very far from

Reception of the ambassadors of Siam by Jean-Léon Gérôme

On 27 June 1861 Napoleon III received the ambassadors of Siam in the Salle de Bal.

equalling those made by the cabinet-maker in his youth. In 1979 the Musée
Napoléon Premier was created in the château, with a collection of pictures,
sculptures and objects of exceptional quality given to the State by Prince Napoleon
and his sister, the Comtesse de Witt.

PLACE

The buildings on the Cour Ovale are the oldest part of the château, and were built by Francis I between 1527 and 1535 on the ruins of the medieval castle. This court, more or less oval and originally enclosed, was opened up and renovated by Henri IV in 1606. The redesigned apartments were installed there. The Galerie François Premier wing, built at the same time as the first work was undertaken, was originally just one part of the royal apartments. To the west it joined the Couvent des Mathurins, which was almost entirely rebuilt by Francis I during the same period. The Cour du Cheval Blanc, also built by Francis I, but very much altered later, was initially no more than a servants' courtyard; it was not promoted to a court of honour containing the main entrance, until the second half of the seventeenth century. The building forming the back of the court is the most complicated part.

Its development was impeded by the presence of the monastery, which was demolished stage by stage only between 1535 and 1540. The main building work on the château was virtually finished at the end of Francis I's reign, but the internal furnishing and decoration were not completed until the second half of the sixteenth century and the early years of the seventeenth, at the same time as the exterior was almost completely reclad. It is frustrating that the alterations made in the nineteenth century have made the château more difficult to understand.

The Cour Ovale

The Pavillon de la Porte Dorée • The royal apartments
The so-called Portique de Serlio • The Pavillon des Enfants, the Salle du Guet,
the Pavillon des Dauphins, the Porte du Baptistère,
Saint-Saturnin chapel • The Salle de Bal

The buildings on the Cour Ovale constructed in the period of Francis I were sited on the remains of the medieval castle, the towers and curtain walls of which enclosed a polygonal courtyard. Because the east end was reshaped in the reign of Henri IV the complex today is more horseshoe-shaped than oval, but the court is still known as the Cour Ovale.

The medieval castle contained a large square tower, the *donjon* or Keep, which has been preserved, and round turrets that reinforced each corner of the polygon externally. All these turrets have disappeared, most of them destroyed in Francis I's day, except for two which could still be seen at the end of the sixteenth century. The entrance to the castle was located on the south-west corner, and was protected by a barbican formed by two of these turrets. The entrance has not been moved, but the barbican has been replaced by the Pavillon de la Porte Dorée which provided the entrance to the château until the beginning of the seventeenth century, that is until the main entrance was transferred to the Cour du Cheval Blanc. Since the reign of Francis I a long tree-lined avenue has led up to the Porte Dorée.

The medieval buildings were made of limestone, while those erected by Francis I were made of sandstone, the hard, greyish stone extracted straight from the rocks in the forest. The sandstone is used as quarry-stones which are rendered, except for the corners and the frames round the openings where dressed stones are used. This masonry is characteristic of all the parts erected in the first phase of building work commissioned by Francis I, fulfilling the famous 1528 specification agreed with the master mason Gilles Le Breton. The buildings constructed in the

Cour Ovale

Door of the spiral staircase serving the Salle de Bal and the Pavillon de la Porte Dorée.

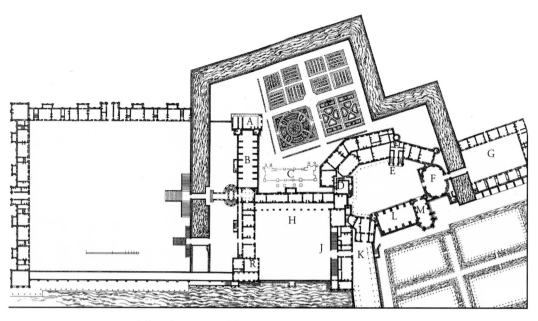

Ground-floor plan, measured drawing by Jacques Androuet Du Cerceau, 1579

A. Pavillon des Armes; B. Trinité church; C. Pergola (destroyed); D. Keep; E. Portique de Serlio;
F. Salle du Guet (destroyed); G. Conciergerie (destroyed); H. Galerie François Premier wing; J. Wing
of the Belle Cheminée; K. Pavillon de la Porte Dorée; L. Salle de Bal wing; M. Saint-Saturnin chapel;
N. Pavillon de la Grotte des Pins; P. Galerie d'Ulysse wing; R. Pavillon des Poêles.

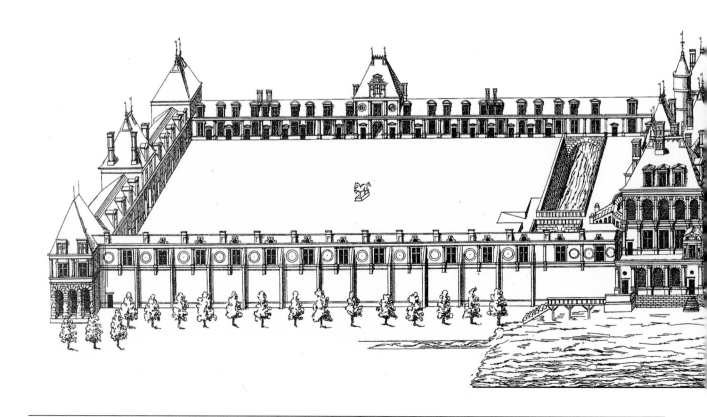

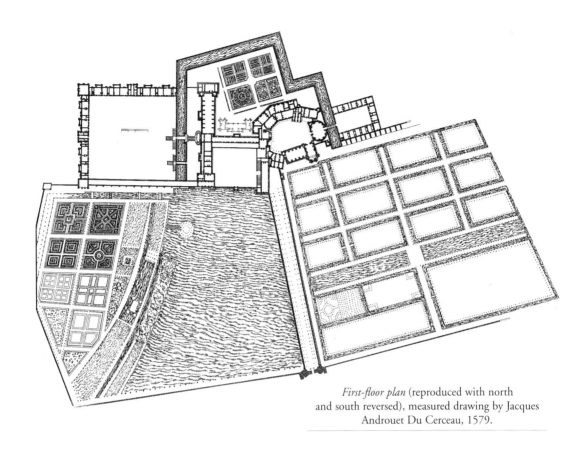

First-floor plan (reproduced with north
and south reversed), measured drawing by Jacques
Androuet Du Cerceau, 1579.

Bird's eye view, taken from the south,
measured drawing by Jacques
Androuet Du Cerceau, 1579.

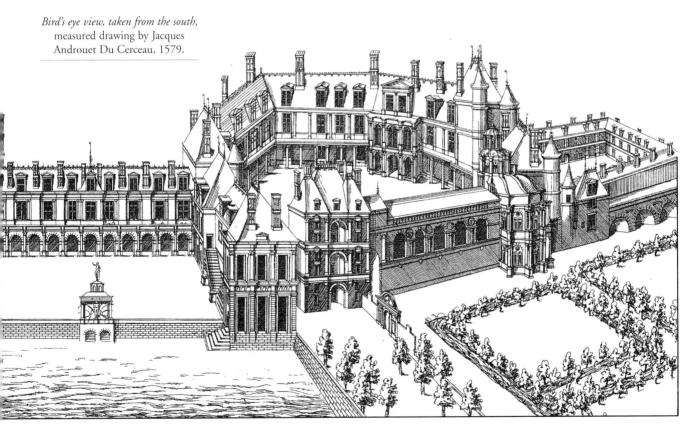

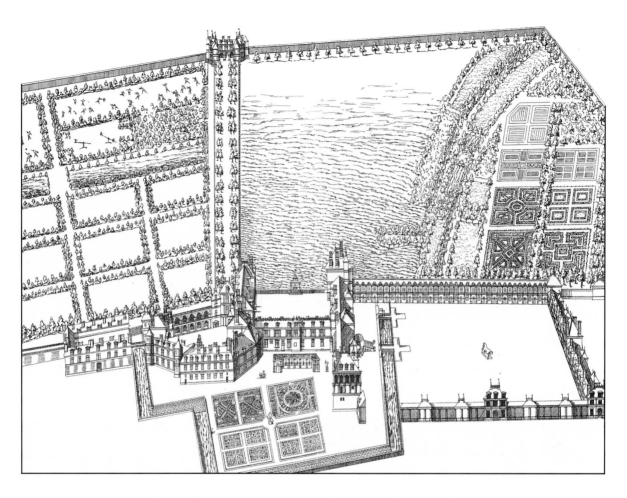

General view of the château, measured drawing by Jacques Androuet Du Cerceau, 1579

Bird's eye view, taken from the north.

reign of Henri IV also used this type of masonry so that they would not stand out from other buildings in the Cour Ovale. The most important areas are made entirely of dressed stone, and date either from Francis I's second building campaign or from Henri IV's.

But for the style, the irregularity of the ground-plan of the court, the way in which materials are used to accentuate certain features and the relative independence of the buildings in relation to one another would have made Francis I's château look like a medieval building. The style comes from the use of regularly spaced pilasters with fanciful capitals, their rhythm broken by the windows spaced at irregular intervals and sometimes placed between two pilasters. These windows were originally casements, that is, divided by stone mullions and window bars. This is still the style at Chambord. In the most important areas the

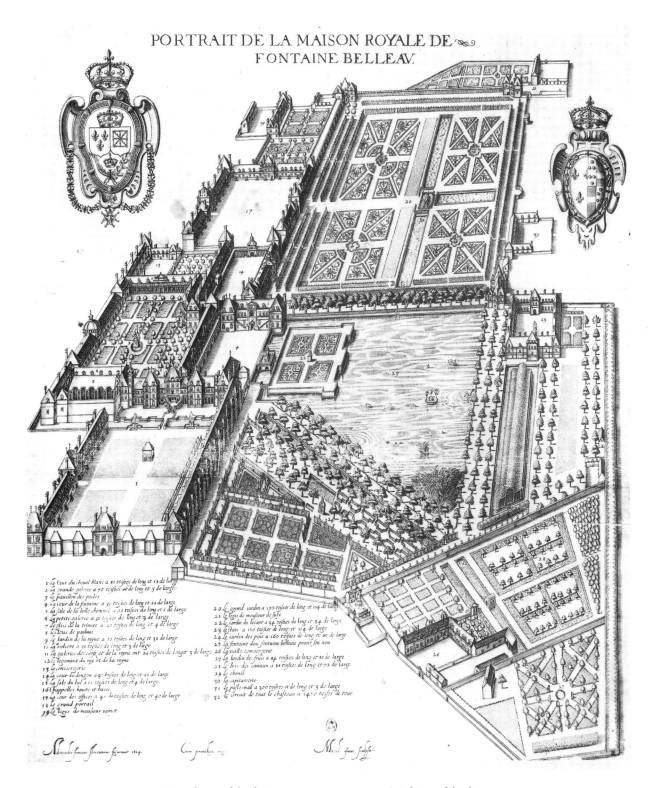

PORTRAIT DE LA MAISON ROYALE DE
FONTAINE BELLEAV.

General view of the château

This drawing by Alexandre Francine, engraved
by Michel Lasne in 1614, shows a bird's-eye
view taken from the west.

Aerial view of the château

Following pages:
General view of the château and the outlying
buildings taken from the south-east.

Capitals in the Cour Ovale, measured drawing by Rodolphe Pfnor, 1863

Capital in the keep with the "F" of Francis I; capital in the Pavillon des Dauphins; capital with the cipher "HM" (Henri IV and Marie de' Medici).

Cour Ovale

Wing between the Pavillon de la Porte Dorée and the Keep.

Cour Ovale

Double page over: Left, the Pavillon de la Porte Dorée; right, the Keep.

Cour Ovale

In the foreground,
the Portique de Serlio.

Cour Ovale

In this engraving made by Jacques Rigaud in 1738
the Porte du Baptistère can be seen in the background.

pilasters are replaced by columns, but their capitals still belong to the old reper-
tory, the flamboyant style of the Loire which has its roots in the Middle Ages.

It is surprising that the Renaissance king who built the hunting châteaux of
Chambord and Madrid following a regular plan should have made do with this
picturesque garland of pavilions or wings, one forming each side of the polygon.
It was thought that Francis I wanted to honour the layout of a castle that Louis
IX, the patron saint of the Capetian dynasty, had sanctified, but the explanation
lies elsewhere. Chambord and Madrid were châteaux intended for hunting and
short stays, built from scratch following plans that could be described as playful,
and designed for social activities as well as intellectual ones. Fontainebleau was a
royal residence. Due to economic factors, which the king had to consider like any
of his subjects, and the public's attachment to tradition and custom, most of the
large Renaissance châteaux are little more than old châteaux dressed up as new. It
was only gradually that the demand for regularity made its mark in France.

The Pavillon de la Porte Dorée is described at length in the 1528 specification,
which was followed closely during construction. The main part, covered by a high

Small view painted as a fresco in the Galerie François Premier

This view shows the château c. 1540.
From left to right: the Galerie
François Premier wing,
the Keep (in the background),
the Pavillon de la Porte Dorée,
the wing later replaced by
the Salle de Bal wing. Another later
transformation: the building
of the wing of the Belle Cheminée,
separating the Galerie François
Premier wing from the Pavillon
de la Porte Dorée.

Pavillon de la Porte Dorée

This pavilion with its gilded porch
was one of the first buildings erected
at Fontainebleau by Francis I.

pavilion-style roof, is flanked by two square turrets containing small rooms (one above the other) that frame open areas, the porch on the ground floor and loggias on the upper floors. The interior was decorated with frescoes by Primaticcio, which now are either worn away or incorrectly restored. The superimposition of one loggia above another is based on Italian models, no doubt the Castello Nuovo in Naples and the castle at Urbino, two buildings that the French knew well and admired, and which had also been a source of inspiration at the château of Gaillon. At Fontainebleau the only innovation was the use of small pediments above the windows, doubtless among the first to be seen in France. At both Gaillon and Fontainebleau, the Italian references were full of Gallic touches: the vertical emphasis of the bays, the pavilion roof, the basket arches over the openings in the porch and the loggias. The basket, or *anse de panier,* an arch with several centres is characteristic of French fifteenth and sixteenth-century architecture – an Italian would have used a semi-circular arch instead. "We were dealing with one of those large low doorways, in the bad taste of the French," Cellini wrote, after Francis I had entrusted him with the door ornamentation. "The almost square opening was surmounted by a basket arch." Cellini then came up with a tympanum depicting the nymph of Fontainebleau, and two victories for the spandrels which ended up at Anet – no doubt because they did not fit in at Fontainebleau – as well as two satyrs in the form of piers. "I corrected the opening," Cellini went on, "by giving it superb proportions and above it I placed a perfect semi-circle."[1]

This criticism from a distinguished representative of modern Italian style is a significant factor in the debate over who created the pavilion. It is true that Gilles Le Breton, who never travelled, could not have come up with the Italian model alone. But it is so roughly reproduced that the scheme probably never took any other written form than the 1528 specification, the broad outlines of which may have been dictated by the king himself with Pierre Paule as an intermediary. As already explained, Paule supervised the work carried out under Francis I until his death in 1535. Another name that has been put forward in this connection is that of Girolamo della Robbia. Francis I had commissioned a large ceramic tondo from him for the doorway which was never, like Cellini's tympanum, spandrels and piers, installed. If Girolamo della Robbia was the architect of the château of Madrid in the Bois de Boulogne, built at the same time as Fontainebleau (a skilful design if a little old-fashioned in relation to the Roman taste of the day), the ceramicist cannot have designed the Pavillon de la Porte Dorée, which is even more old-fashioned.

Going round the Cour Ovale in a clockwise direction, after the Pavillon de la Porte Dorée you discover two small buildings. The Escalier du Roi in the first building, added in the eighteenth century, is worth mentioning since it transformed the bedchamber of the Duchess of Étampes into a landing, while respecting the decoration devised by Primaticcio from 1541.

After this comes the Keep, in which the main twelfth-century building work was respected, but covered over. A large pavilion roof covered with slates replaced a roof which, according to written records, was tiled, implying that the pitch was less steep. Pavilion roofs probably first appeared in French architecture in the fourteenth century, and characterised it until the mid-seventeenth century. The Keep is served by a half-projecting spiral staircase, and along with the spiral staircase serving the Pavillon de la Porte Dorée and the wing containing the Salle de Bal, this is one of the last vestiges of the original arrangements for vertical circulation within the château; each corner of the internal perimeter of the court had once contained a round turret with a spiral staircase. These turrets were reputedly added at the time of Francis I, but the principle of access from one level to the next by means of a projecting spiral staircase, with each section of the building being served by its own staircase, goes back to the fifteenth century, or even the fourteenth. Therefore it is believed that these turrets were built at the same time as the turrets fortifying the exterior of the medieval castle, with both being added in the early fifteenth century when work was carried out for Isabeau of Bavaria.

According to a tradition which is no doubt true, the first-floor bedroom in the Keep had been the room occupied by the king ever since the castle had been founded. Francis I first allowed his mother to use it, but moved into it on her death in 1531 when he had the room decorated by Primaticcio. The Galerie François Premier wing was grafted on to the Keep, as described in the 1528 specification. The first-floor gallery decorated by Rosso was the main room of the royal apartment. On the ground floor there was the Appartement des Bains.

Apart from the gallery and the bedchamber in the Keep, the royal apartments included a room preceding the bedchamber (still following a clockwise direction) and an enfilade of rooms in the two following wings. There were two suites of rooms in all, one following the other, with windows facing on to the court: the apartment with the bedchamber in the Keep which Francis I occupied from 1531, and the apartment he had occupied up until then which became the queen's apartment. The bedchamber vacated by the king was then decorated by Primaticcio for Queen Eleanor. The purpose of the rooms in the two apartments – each the depth of a single room – remained the same until the end of the sixteenth century, and was not affected by the creation in Henri II's reign of the royal apartment on the Cour de la Fontaine, which remained unfinished. However, the doubling of the depth of these wings at the end of the sixteenth century by the addition of rooms that overlooked the Jardin de Diane altered the layout drastically. The cross wall separating the rooms overlooking the court from those overlooking the garden was the old curtain wall of the medieval castle. In the seventeenth-century arrangement, the two royal apartments still followed one another in the same order, but they now had rooms overlooking the court and rooms overlooking the garden.

Along the whole ground floor of the areas just described, from the Pavillon de la Porte Dorée onwards, there is a portico with columns, covered to form a terrace, built c. 1531 in the second phase of Francis I's building work. Under the portico a few remains of the fifteenth-century openings can still be seen. This portico meant that people could walk around the courtyard under cover, and provided the terrace above for horizontal circulation along the first floor, which had hitherto been dependent on the interconnection of communicating rooms.

Adding the portico around the periphery meant removing the medieval spiral staircases. A new means of vertical circulation within the building had to be provided. That is what the flight of steps and the staircase that supplanted it, one in front of and the other behind the projecting bay inappropriately called the Portique de Serlio, were used for. Excavations revealed that in front of this projecting bay there was an uncovered external double flight of steps which allowed access to the

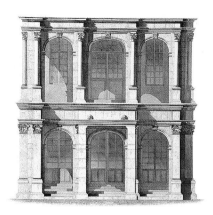

Portique de Serlio, measured drawing
by Rodolphe Pfnor, 1863

This drawing shows a stage prior
to the rebuilding – wrongly described as
a restoration – carried out by Boitte in 1882.

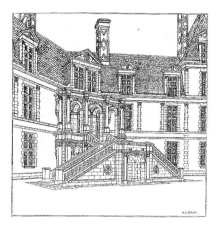

*External steps in front of
the portico*

The external steps
that originally went
with the portico were
destroyed c. 1540.
This drawing is
a reconstruction
by Albert Bray made
in 1946.

*Exercise in perspective
by Sebastiano Serlio*

To present this purely
theoretical exercise
published in *Il secundo
libro di prospettiva*
in 1545, Serlio seems
to have made a measured
drawing of the external
steps before they were
destroyed.

first floor. In a medieval French residence a flight of steps that provided direct access
to the first floor indicated a site of power or a royal residence, like the steps in the
palace on the Ile de la Cité in Paris. The flight of steps in the Cour Ovale had only
a short-lived existence, from 1531 to 1541. It had been designed to provide a grand
entrance to the bedchamber first used by the king, but no sooner was it finished
than the king moved into the bedchamber in the Keep. The symbolism was then at
odds with itself. However, the decision to demolish this new feature and replace it
by a more discreet internal staircase was not taken until 1541[2]. It was intended to
serve both the apartment relinquished to the queen and the Pavillon des Enfants
Royaux which ran along the Cour Ovale from the staircase. When work on Henri
IV's project to open up the court to the east was in progress, the projecting bay had
to be pivoted around on itself and realigned. The staircase had to follow suit. The
question is whether the staircase built in Francis I's reign was therefore retained, and
merely pivoted around too. This is quite credible, as Abbé Guilbert writing in 1731
described it as being adorned with "pilasters and columns of a composite Gothic

Lamp base in the first-floor loggia of the Portique de Serlio

This is one of the few vestiges of the ornamental work dating from the time
of Francis I spared by the 1882 restoration.

order"[3], a description that fits in well with the work carried out in Francis I's reign. In 1748 this staircase that dated partly from the sixteenth, partly from the seventeenth century, was replaced by the Escalier de la Reine, similar in style to the Escalier du Roi, constructed at the same time[4].

The 1531 flight of steps was constructed by Gilles Le Breton. The "Portique de Serlio" of which the steps were an integral part (it can clearly be seen where they have been torn out) therefore predates Serlio's arrival at Fontainebleau in 1541. It is therefore no longer possible to attribute it to the Bolognese architect, as has long been the case. But the name of a great master, even if it has been used apocryphally, is hard to eradicate. The reconstruction of the flight of steps suggested by Albert Bray, who was in charge of the excavations, may be unconsciously inspired by a flight of steps in Serlio's Book II. Or maybe the drawing in Book II, devoted to perspective and published in Paris in 1545, is a drawing of the flight of steps at Fontainebleau, done for the sole purpose of illustrating an exercise in perspective.

The attribution of the portico to Serlio goes back a long way, so it has become customary to see the projecting bay as a sort of triumphal arch directly derived from the archaeology of the day, as published by Serlio in *Le antiquità di Roma* in 1540. But where has a triumphal arch with a design like this ever been seen? Where can any application of the canonical rules be seen in this façade where the columns are on the second level, and the capitals and basket arches are in the same vein as the Pavillon de la Porte Dorée? How is it possible that it was designed by a great master such as Rosso who had seen Bramante's *tempietto* in Rome and who was still in that city which represented all that was modern when it was sacked in 1527? The only difference between the projecting bay and the parts of the court already described lies in the use of dressed stone; it was built only three years after them. Its half-Italian, half-French design could again be the outcome of collaboration between Pierre Paule and Gilles Le Breton. The internal staircase, on the other hand, of which nothing is known, dated from Serlio's arrival. Perhaps Serlio made the alteration, which would explain why his name has remained associated with the place.

The Pavillon des Enfants, adjacent to the "Portique de Serlio" contained the apartments of the royal children and immediately followed on from the queen's apartment. It was built in accordance with the 1528 specification. In Henri IV's day it was rebuilt more or less identically, but farther to the east so that the Cour Ovale could be opened up, an event usually dated between 1601 and 1606. The Pavillon des Enfants continued to be used for the same purpose until the end of the *Ancien Régime*.

Following on from it, in Francis I's day, was a building containing the Salle du Guet, which can be quite clearly seen on Androuet Du Cerceau's measured drawing. Even the most highly qualified authors to have written about the château of Fontainebleau have given up any attempt to retrace the complicated history of this short-lived building. However, it is possible to clear up a few misunderstandings today[5].

Androuet Du Cerceau depicts it as a rectangular building, its corners rounded on the inside to form a more or less oval room[6]. The 1528 specification provided for the reconstruction of the "large tumble-down block to make a Salle du Guet"[7]. This block was apparently the ruins of the great medieval hall. It was traditional to use the great hall of a castle both for the *guet* (the watch) and for unusually large receptions. The watch, or garrison, usually occupied the room and vacated it for festivities[8].

The Salle du Guet was Francis I's ceremonial or banqueting hall. (It is known that the gallery was not used in this way.) The Salle du Guet must have been used to receive Emperor Charles V in December 1539. And it was probably also there that the christening of the future Francis II took place in 1544, and that of Elisabeth of France in 1546. The christening of Élisabeth, the daughter of the then Dauphin, subsequently Henri II, was a particularly solemn occasion because it coincided with the conclusion of the peace treaty between Francis I and Henry VIII of England, who had agreed to be the princess's godfather and had sent his representative to the ceremony.

The many witnesses at the ceremony wrote of temporary structures, an "antique-style theatre", and a "newly renovated room", which many Fontainebleau historians thought was in the middle of the court – in fact, it was probably the Salle du Guet, temporarily transformed. It is this transformation that led people to describe a room which had been built or rebuilt in accordance with the 1528 specification as "new". If the transformation dated back to the reception for Charles V, its possible attribution to Serlio would have to be abandoned, as will become clear.

It is thought that the transformation was carried out for the christening of the future Francis II in 1544. The room would thus have been used for the christening ceremony of several royal children: three Bourbons as well as the two Valois, since on 15 September 1606, the Dauphin – the future Louis XIII (then five years old) – and his two sisters Élisabeth and Chrétienne were christened at Fontainebleau. The original intention had been for the baptism to take place at Notre-Dame in Paris but, to escape an epidemic, Henri IV suddenly decided to

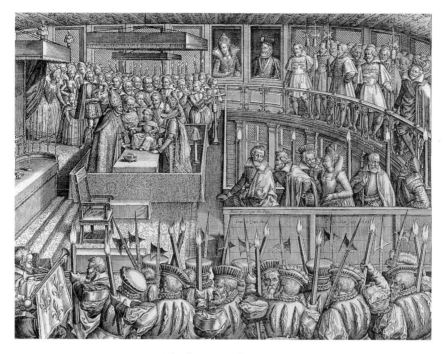

The christening of Louis XIII

On this engraving by Léonard Gaultier after a drawing by Jean Le Clerc, King Henri IV
and his queen, Marie de' Medici can be seen at the top, in the middle. The christening took
place in 1606 in the Salle du Guet, probably designed by Serlio in the 1540s,
then destroyed to make room for the gate known as the Porte du Baptistère.

hold the ceremony at Fontainebleau, a healthy place of refuge during outbreaks of
plague or cholera. The christening ceremony of Louis XIII, depicted by Léonard
Gaultier, has always been seen as taking place in a temporary building erected in
the courtyard, but it is only necessary to look at Gaultier's engraving alongside
Androuet Du Cerceau's to realise that this is in fact the same Salle du Guet with
its rounded corners[9]. A justification for the choice of this room for the
christening ceremonies in 1544, 1546 and 1606 would have been its proximity to
the Pavillon des Enfants.

The attribution of the transformation of the Salle du Guet to Serlio is
supported by the presence of several oval antique-style rooms in the work of the
Bolognese artist, particularly in his scheme for a "palazzo del principe illustrissimo
nela [sic] città", which has usually been identified as a scheme for the Louvre. Yet
another argument can be advanced in support of this attribution. It is probably on
the site of the Salle du Guet and not in the Salle de Bal that the scheme for a
loggia published by Serlio in his Book VII[10] should be located. This scheme
included a low hall on the ground floor for which Serlio again used the idea of

rounded corners and in which he arranged recesses to house the bronzes made by Primaticcio and copied from antique statues. The antique-style theatre (an allusion to the Roman amphitheatre) would thus have housed statues after the antique. According to Androuet Du Cerceau's plan drawings, the Salle du Guet already had recesses of this kind; the first floor was a loggia.

Therefore the Salle du Guet was not destroyed until after the christening in September 1606, and all the building work carried out in Henri IV's reign to open up the court, dated between 1601 and 1606, could not have been completed until the last three months of 1606. This complex included mainly the new Pavillon des Enfants, a new identical, symmetrical pavilion known as the Pavillon des Dauphins, linking buildings joining these pavilions to the parts that had been preserved, an enclosing wall and finally the Porte du Baptistère, the only part that is seventeenth century in style. In fact the design of the façades dating from Francis I's time was repeated throughout, showing a concern for homogeneity of style which deserves to be emphasised. The historical circumstances just detailed as well as the iconography of the decor using dolphins (*dauphins*) explain the name given to this doorway, the Porte du Baptistère or the Porte Dauphine, as well as that given to the Pavillon des Dauphins.

Saint-Saturnin chapel comes next in the court tour – a double chapel containing two chapels, one on the lower level and one on the first floor. This arrangement is reminiscent of the plan of the Sainte-Chapelle which belonged to the palace on the Ile de la Cité in Paris and of several other royal or princely chapels. The upper chapel was reserved for the master of the house and his family while the lower

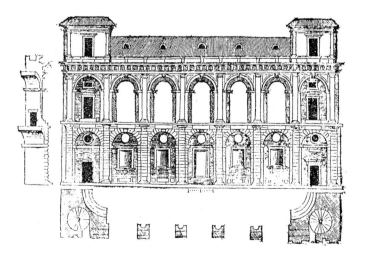

Scheme for a wing with a loggia by Sebastiano Serlio

Published in 1575 in Book VII (published posthumously), this scheme probably dates from 1552–1554. The wing was intended to replace the Salle du Guet.

View taken from the Cour des Offices

Double page over:
From left to right: the Pavillon des Dauphins, the Porte du Baptistère, the Pavillon des Enfants.

The Porte du Baptistère, exterior view, detail

The lower part of this gateway was reused,
and came from the gateway constructed
by Primaticcio in the Cour du Cheval Blanc.

The Porte du Baptistère, exterior view

In the foreground, one of the terms from
the entrance into the Cour des Offices,
carved by Gilles Guérin in 1640.

chapel was used by his officials and servants. Built in dressed stone and less enclosed by other buildings than it is today, it appeared as the pendant of the "Portique de Serlio" and shared with it many "French" features including basket arches and fanciful capitals, featuring the Fontainebleau stag. It is generally accepted that the two buildings date from the same period (the 1528 specification simply provided space for the chapel), but the date of the start of work on the chapel is given as 1541, whereas the correct date is probably 1531, which is in fact the date of the portico. Confusion has arisen because of the Latin inscription that appears on the high vaulting, translated as "Francis, King of France, completed it in 1545" [11], but the interior furnishing may have delayed completion of the building. The

*Capitals on the Porte
du Baptistère,*
measured drawing
by Rodolphe Pfnor, 1863

The dolphins (*dauphins*)
on the capital are a reminder
of the christening
of the Dauphin,
subsequently Louis XIII.

The Porte du Baptistère, interior view from inside the Cour Ovale

This gateway, also known as the Porte Dauphine, was built on
the site of the room in which the Dauphin was baptised in 1606.

superimposition of columns above pilasters, which could be justified on the portico only by the presence of the flight of steps, is repeated in the apse of the chapel. This superimposition, so contrary to the canons of order, is used to indicate hierarchy, the columns being used only on the upper floor reserved for the king. It seems out of the question that any of this work could be by Serlio, to whom the chapel has been attributed. The building was the work of Gilles Le Breton, perhaps still directed by Pierre Paule.

The chapel was later hemmed in by the wing containing the Salle de Bal (built in the reigns of Francis I and Henri II) and the wing built in the reign of Henri IV between the Pavillon des Dauphins and the chapel, with a façade that overlooked the court – as had the façade of the Salle de Bal. Henri IV's architect, who usually showed better judgement, extended the façade across the front of the chapel, causing it to lose its original façade, which can be seen on Androuet Du Cerceau's engraving. The side windows of the upper chapel were turned into blind windows for the same reason.

The wing containing the Salle de Bal, lying between the chapel and the Pavillon de la Porte Dorée, rounds off the tour. The 1528 specification for this site envisaged the construction of a wing containing the pantries, kitchens and a "revestière" (sacristy) for the chapel, with a gallery on the upper floor. This wing can be seen in the small painted view in the Galerie François Premier[12], and it is not known precisely when it was replaced, although the contract for the woodwork

Vaulting over the Porte du Baptistère

This vaulting bears the monogram "HM", for Henri IV
and Marie de' Medici.

Saint-Saturnin chapel

The upper part of Saint-Saturnin chapel seen here from
the Grand Jardin. From left to right: the Salle de Bal;
Saint-Saturnin upper chapel; the Pavillon des Dauphins.

on the floors and roof dates only from 13 July 1548[13], and by then Francis I was
dead. De l'Orme had been commissioned by Henri II to check the work carried out
by Gilles Le Breton in the lifetime of the late king. Le Breton had built a wing
containing lodgings[14] on the ground floor, and a narrow room on the first floor
enclosed on either side by a sequence of open bays, overlooking the court and the
garden. This arrangement of open bays was the same as that used at Blois and the
château of Madrid, and in the Pavillon de la Porte Dorée. Le Breton subsequently
integrated these bays into the internal space of the room. The explanation given for
this move was the desire to widen an excessively narrow room (almost a gallery) so as
to turn it into a large hall intended ultimately to replace the Salle du Guet.

As already said, De l'Orme replaced the vaulting Le Breton had built over the
room with a wooden floor from which a coffered ceiling was suspended. Not only had
he found faults in the masonry work that threatened the stability of the wing, but the
barrel vault constructed by Le Breton was based on a basket arch, a shape frowned

Saint-Saturnin chapel, cross-section,
measured drawing
by Rodolphe Pfnor, 1863

This cross-section shows the two
superimposed chapels jointly
described as Saint-Saturnin.
The Cour Ovale is on the right.

Saint-Saturnin chapel, capitals,
measured drawing
by Rodolphe Pfnor, 1863

The capitals of the upper chapel feature
the stag and the "F" of Francis I.

on by the Italians and one which the French ceased to use from the reign of Henri II onwards. Thus the last demonstration of the "bad taste" of Le Breton or the person specifying his work was eliminated. The passage from Serlio's Book VII in which he praises De l'Orme's approach and laments the fact that De l'Orme's scheme was chosen in preference to his own scheme for a loggia has already been quoted.

While it is true that Serlio's name, which can be followed all the way round the court, has remained attached only to the Salle du Guet, its short-lived transformation and the scheme for the loggia which was not carried out, it crops up again in the Cour du Cheval Blanc.

The Cour du Cheval blanc

The destruction of the Couvent des Mathurins
The building forming the back of the court • The wings of the court •
The horse, the moat, the Jeu de Paume

Coming from the Cour Ovale, where the layout battles with its medieval past, and entering the Cour du Cheval Blanc, which at first glance seems regular enough, the impression is that the château's tumultuous origins have been left behind and that history will henceforth follow a steadier course. In fact the information provided by source material and the accounts for the royal buildings are as plentiful as they are murky, and are no longer bound up with the irregularities of the buildings. Just when the outline of one building seems to be identified, the building in question is its predecessor, neighbour or counterpart.

Most of the building work carried out between 1527 and 1535, other than the work on the Cour Ovale, related to the restoration and enlargement of the Couvent des Mathurins, which is no longer in existence. The fact that Francis I was sufficiently interested in it to buy back the land belonging to the monastery in 1529[1] does not necessarily mean that he already had a scheme for a large west court in mind. The restoration work undertaken on the old castle obviously called for work of the same order in the monastery, which could on occasion serve as a makeshift lodging for the king while the building work on the Cour Ovale was in progress. From 1 August 1527 to 5 June 1528, Le Breton had been required to construct new buildings "for the king within the abbey of Fontainebleau, working hard day and night, because of the arrival" of the king, Louise of Savoy and the king and queen of Navarre. The official inspection of this first building phase was carried out on 28 August 1528 by Pierre Paule, the first time his name is mentioned in the royal accounts[2]. In the 1528 specification Le Breton undertook

Cour du Cheval Blanc

This detail of the horseshoe-shaped flight of steps shows a caduceus.

165

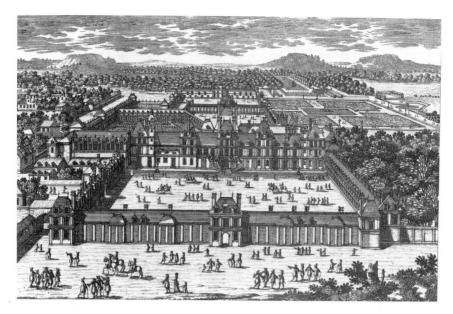

Cour du Cheval Blanc

This engraving by Aveline which dates from the second half of the seventeenth century
is the only view showing the wing enclosing the court, destroyed in the reign of Napoleon I.

Cour du Cheval Blanc, building forming the back of the court, measured drawing
by Jacques Androuet Du Cerceau, 1579

From left to right: the Pavillon des Armes with the Tour de l'Horloge; the Trinité church with the
Pavillon des Orgues at its side; the Pavillon du Vestibule with the horseshoe-shaped flight of steps;
the queen-mothers' wing with the Unnamed Pavilion at its side; the Pavillon des Poêles. In the
foreground, the moat and the bridges installed by Primaticcio in 1565. On the right, the gateway
that would be reused in the Porte du Baptistère.

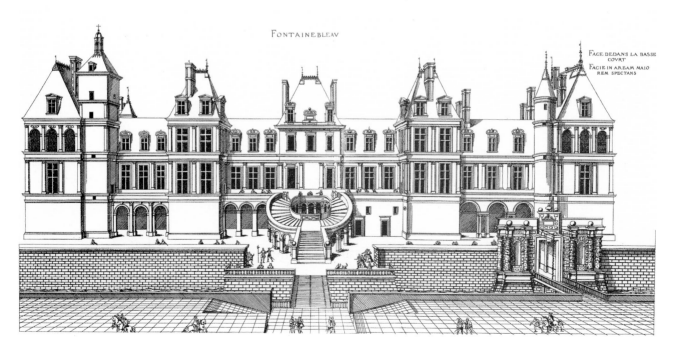

Arrival of Louis XIV in the Cour du Cheval Blanc

This engraving by Israël Sylvestre reconstructs Louis XIV's arrival at Fontainebleau in 1667,
with the château now entered via the horseshoe-shaped flight of steps.

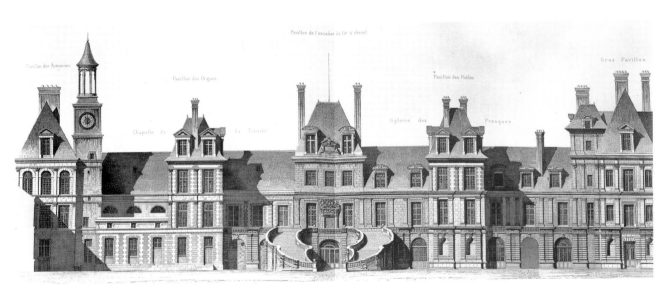

Cour du Cheval Blanc, buildings forming the back of the court,
measured drawing by Rodolphe Pfnor, 1863

Following pages: *Cour du Cheval Blanc*

The present state hardly differs from its appearance in 1863.
A comparison with Androuet Du Cerceau's drawing, on the other hand, reveals major differences.

Cour du Cheval Blanc, buildings forming the back of the court

From left to right: the Pavillon des Armes with the Tour de l'Horloge;
the Pavillon des Orgues alongside the Trinité church;
the Pavillon du Vestibule with the horseshoe-shaped flight of steps.

both to restore "the old residential buildings of the abbey" and to "construct a new building as a lodging for the monks"[3]. On 7 September 1527 a carpentry contract was agreed for "two residential buildings and open galleries forming a square [...] in the yard of the abbey". The official inspection of that new work was carried out in 1531, and payments made in 1535[4]. These references relate to the wings and galleries of a cloister and not, as has been suggested, to the wings of the Cour du Cheval Blanc. What may have led to this mistake is the fact that the monastery was razed bit by bit in 1535–1540, falling victim to two circumstances, the completion of work on the residential accommodation on the Cour Ovale for the king's accommodation, and his ambition to enlarge the château.

The building along the back of the court is the part of Fontainebleau that raises more questions than any other. Its chronology is uncertain, its composition

Cour du Cheval Blanc, buildings forming the back of the court

From left to right: the Pavillon du Vestibule with the horseshoe-shaped flight of steps;
the Unnamed Pavilion alongside the queen-mothers' wing;
far right, the Pavillon Louis XV, the start of the Louis XV wing.

complex, its masonry varied, the names given to its different parts unclear, and its position in the château as a whole ambiguous. At the north and south ends the principal façade is at the back, facing north on to the Jardin de Diane and south on to the Cour de la Fontaine. Going from north to south, it is made up of the Pavillon des Armes, the Trinité church with the Pavillon des Orgues beside it, the Pavillon du Vestibule, the queen-mothers' wing with an unnamed pavilion beside it, and lastly the Pavillon des Poêles – or to be more precise the remains of it, sacrificed as it was to the Gros Pavillon which can be seen only from the Cour de la Fontaine.

In the 1537–1540 accounts there are payments (similarly unspecific) to painters and stucco artists for work done "in the large room of the pavilion recently built anew near the pond [...] where the stoves are to be placed"[(5)].

There can be no doubt as to its identification: this is the pavilion that would be named the Pavillon des Poêles: its main façades overlooked the Étang and the Cour de la Fontaine, and only its small side could be seen from the Cour du Cheval Blanc. According to tradition, it was in this pavilion that Emperor Charles V lodged during his stay at Fontainebleau in December 1539. The theory that there was a link between that visit and the stoves is valid. Closed stoves were unknown in sixteenth-century France; French travellers going eastwards were astonished to see them in every abode from Strasbourg to Moscow. The first stoves, imported from Germany, made their appearance in France's royal residences in around 1520, and their presence at Fontainebleau illustrates Francis I's desire to make this pavilion "in the German style"[6]. This was certainly a courtesy towards his guest.

Some claim that the pavilion could not have been built when the emperor's arrival became known, but in fact the text quoted suggests a pavilion already built and stoves that had not yet arrived. If the construction of the pavilion itself is dated to c. 1535, the theory would not be far out. However, there is no precise description of what it looked like, and its appearance cannot be confused with that shown on Androuet Du Cerceau's measured drawing since in the meantime, c. 1560, it was given a new external cladding by Primaticcio.

The building of the Pavillon des Orgues and the Unnamed Pavilion can be associated with the work carried out in the 1530s. All the characteristic features of the first buildings on the Cour Ovale are repeated here: rendered sandstone walls, rectangular casements, dormer windows with a triangular pediment, pilasters with a capital marked with the "F" of Francis I. It is impossible to continue to insist that the first pavilion was built in the reign of Henri II and the second in that of Charles IX. Two low wings joined the Pavillon des Orgues to the Unnamed Pavilion and the Unnamed Pavilion to the Pavillon des Poêles: the remains of one of these is still present near the Pavillon des Orgues. The alignment of these wings and pavilions, characterised by sandstone masonry, was not the beginning of a large western court. The main thrust was southwards, towards the Étang in which the Pavillon des Poêles was reflected; thus the future Cour de la Fontaine was beginning to take shape near the Étang.

Developing the alignment northwards entailed the destruction of the monastery. The Pavillon des Armes, given its name because the royal armoury was kept there, is undated. It cannot have been built before the monastery was destroyed since it is built on one of the cloister galleries that was preparing to be roofed over in 1527. Three arches in the style of the 1520–1530 period can be seen at the foot of the south wall of the pavilion, and it is thought that they are remains of that gallery. The pavilion itself is almost entirely constructed in dressed sandstone, and the loggias have semi-circular openings that are characteristic of the latest building work on the Cour Ovale, the wing containing the Salle de Bal. Its strange Egyptian-style door facing the Jardin de Diane still sports the "F" of Francis I. For these reasons its construction can probably be dated to the 1540s.

It was also at that time that the idea of the western court gained a hold: the Pavillon des Armes to the north was conceived as the pendant to the Pavillon des Poêles. Yet the fact that the two pavilions strongly resemble one another on Androuet Du Cerceau's measured drawing does not necessarily mean that the Pavillon des Armes was a copy of the Pavillon des Poêles, for as already explained the latter was reclad in the 1560s by Primaticcio; that cladding was perhaps intended to make it match the Pavillon des Armes, meaning that only the latter was original.

Next to the Pavillon des Armes are two square towers, one on the garden side, the other on the court side. The one on the garden side houses the spiral staircase serving the pavilion, and the Egyptian door allows access to it. The tower on the court side, obviously made to house a spiral staircase (the stairwell remained empty), eventually became home to the château clock. An outside clock was mentioned at Fontainebleau as early as 1532[7], but its location is uncertain. A second one was installed in the Cour Ovale in 1539[8]. Apparently it was only in 1642, after its height had been extended, that the tower on the Cour du Cheval Blanc became home to the main clock of the château, and came to be known as the Tour de l'Horloge[9].

The presence of two towers intended to house a spiral staircase adjoining the same pavilion is intriguing, and can be more easily explained if we identify the Tour de l'Horloge with the bell-tower of the former Couvent des Mathurins. It is between these two towers that the three arches already mentioned can be seen. The church of the former monastery, which must have had the usual orientation, that is with the apse to the east, was borded on its north side by the cloister, and by the Pavillon des Orgues[10] on its south side.

The Trinité church does not have the usual orientation. It incorporated the wing adjacent to the Pavillon des Orgues built by Le Breton, which became the first part of its nave. When the old church was destroyed, the nave was extended as far as the Pavillon des Armes and side chapels, covered with terraces[11], were built along its entire length on either side, facing on to the court and the garden. These terraces made horizontal circulation along the façades at first-floor level possible. On the court side they passed through the Pavillon des Orgues, where the church's organ had been installed, giving the building its name. These

Cour du Cheval Blanc

This engraving by Israël Sylvestre dating from the mid-seventeenth century highlights the existence of a fountain which backed on to the parapet running along the moat. On the left, the Pavillon du Vestibule with the horseshoe-shaped flight of steps; on the right, the Galerie d'Ulysse wing.

The horseshoe-shaped flight of steps

This engraving by Israël Sylvestre shows the flight of steps in the Cour du Cheval Blanc from an unusual angle, a view from underneath one of the flight rises.

arrangements, which subsequently underwent so many alterations that it is no longer possible to follow them today, were implemented during Henri II's reign by Philibert De l'Orme who in 1551 commissioned the roof timbers for the church "ready to be built anew"[12]. In 1554 he commissioned the interior furnishing of the church[13].

The construction of the Pavillon du Vestibule (this name is not recognised, but it is more eloquent than that usually given to it, the Pavillon des Peintures) is attributed to Primaticcio in the reign of Charles IX, because of an inscription on the top which bears the date 1565. But it was started earlier, not in the time of Francis I as his bust adorning the door might lead us to believe (the bust was added by restorers working for Louis-Philippe who were very fond of playing tricks and laying snares!), but at the very end of Henri II's reign. The king's accidental death in 1559 prevented De l'Orme from completing the transfer of the main entrance of the château from the Porte Dorée to a vestibule allowing direct access to the Trinité church, the Galerie François Premier and the queen-mothers' apartment. The building of the vestibule which was to be inserted into the wing that Le Breton had constructed between the Pavillon des Orgues and the Unnamed Pavilion was envisaged in the masonry contract drawn up on 23 August 1558[14].

In order to provide a terrace in front of the Pavillon du Vestibule, De l'Orme planned to set it back in relation to the alignment of Le Breton's pavilions. To

The horseshoe-shaped flight of steps, measured drawing
by Rodolphe Pfnor, 1863

These steps were built by Jean Androuet Du Cerceau in 1632, partly reusing
the flight built by Philibert de l'Orme in the mid-sixteenth century.

Following pages: *The horseshoe-
shaped flight of steps*

provide access to the terrace he planned to build a flight of steps which would symbolically replace the one in the Cour Ovale as the site of the royal entrance. Only the flight of steps was built, and it was a masterpiece of stone-cutting, admired for the complexity of its vaulting, which followed the form of a horseshoe, or *fer à cheval,* after which it was named. The name was transferred to the flight of steps built by Jean Androuet Du Cerceau in 1632 to replace De l'Orme's which was on the verge of collapse[15].

De l'Orme had also intended to use limestone instead of sandstone as a building material. Saint-Leu stone, a limestone from Saint-Leu-d'Esserent (Oise) transported all over the Ile de France by the river network based on the Seine, made it possible to produce those fine bonds of dressed stones with close joints which De l'Orme advocated. Moreover it introduced a disparity into the texture of the château which De l'Orme's successors, from Primaticcio to Gabriel, tried to mask by covering, without succeeding in cladding completely, the old parts of the building with this stone.

The contract agreed on 23 August 1558 also envisaged the rebuilding or recladding of the wing which came to be known as the queen-mothers' wing when it was occupied by queen-mothers, from Catherine de' Medici to Anne of Austria. The work was carried out solely by Primaticcio who extended it as far as the Pavillon des Poêles. In front of the queen-mothers' wing ran a terrace matching the one running in front of the church: it went through the Unnamed Pavilion just as the other went through the Pavillon des Orgues.

To unify the composition of the building across the whole width of the court, Henri IV's architect covered the ground floor with an arrangement of arched openings, with a semi-circular arch, separated by coupled rusticated pilasters. After unity had been restored in this way, the nineteenth-century architects did their best to destroy it, bringing the façades forward and removing the terraces both between the Pavillon des Armes and the Pavillon des Orgues, and between the Unnamed Pavilion and the Pavillon des Poêles[16].

The long story of the building at the back of the Cour du Cheval Blanc can be summed up as follows: in the 1530s Le Breton restored the monastery, built the Pavillon des Orgues, the Unnamed Pavilion, the Pavillon des Poêles and the intervening wings. The construction of the Pavillon des Armes in the 1540s related to a programme which now made as a priority the creation of a western court. Between 1550 and 1560, both De l'Orme and Primaticcio reworked the complete structure, using limestone in place of sandstone. The undertaking was completed in the seventeenth century and interfered with during the nineteenth century.

Father Dan (1642) and Abbé Guilbert (1731)[17], the first people to write the history of the château of Fontainebleau, attributed the building of the wings on the Cour du Cheval Blanc to Serlio, but dated the start of work ten years before the Bolognese artist arrived. The attribution, which is correct, was abandoned, and the date, which is wrong, was accepted! Léon Palustre, eagerly engaged in the nineteenth century in restoring the claims of the French master masons which, because of the arrogant vanity of the Italian artists, had supposedly been consigned to oblivion, gained credence for a choice that supported his cause[18]. He turned the 1527–1528 texts relating to the Couvent des Mathurins around by attributing them to the wings of the court. His authority went unquestioned, and there was no further attempt to check something that seemed so firmly established. Even Serlio's complaint that he had not been consulted over the Salle de Bal was seen as proof that after being summoned by Francis I he had been left with nothing to do. Serlio seems to have been the victim not of rivalries within the royal workshops between the French and the Italians, or the Florentines and the Bolognese, but of a strange re-play of those rivalries in the works of French historians.

The belated publication of Serlio's Book VI based on two manuscript versions, one held in Munich (1966) and the other in New York (1978), should have turned the tables in Serlio's favour, but this did not happen. Book VI, *Habitationi di tutti li gradi degli homini*, devoted to the dwellings of all classes of men, from the peasant to the king, is valuable testimony to the way in which architectural projects were decided upon in the mid-sixteenth century. For each class Serlio presents a scheme in the Italian manner and a scheme in the French manner, as well as a scheme for the *Casa del re alla campagna*, the king's country residence. The Italian-style residence is a tall villa with a central plan, placed in the middle of a square court surrounded by low buildings; the French-style residence is an elongated main building along a rectangular courtyard with low buildings running round the other three sides. The differences between the two styles and the singularity of the French style were perceived and exploited by Serlio in a remarkable way. His French-style main building is characterised by the tall pavilions and large bays which have already been observed in the Cour Ovale[19].

The publishers of Book VI noticed puzzling similarities between the French-style scheme and the overall appearance of the Cour du Cheval Blanc; but as the immovable milestone of 1528 could not be shifted, they thought that Serlio had copied the Cour du Cheval Blanc to "Frenchify" his scheme. It does not seem very likely that this champion of modernity, summoned to Fontainebleau to alter the way things were being done, would have offered the king something built by a

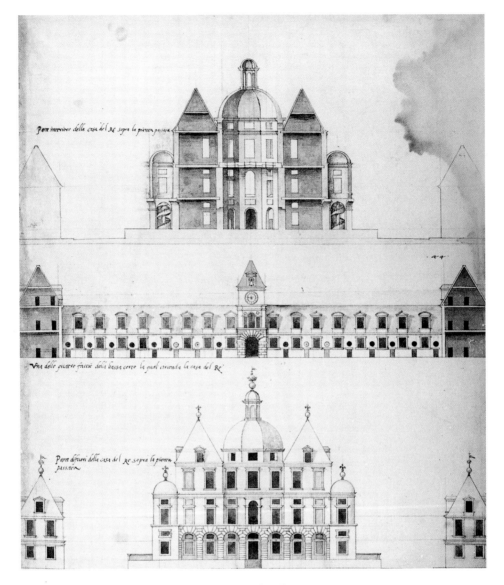

Italian-style scheme by Sebastiano Serlio

This drawing is taken from the manuscript of Serlio's Book VI (New York manuscript).
The scheme shows a main building with a central plan in the middle of the court.

mason ten years earlier. It is strongly believed that the French-style residence in Book VI, altered only as far as required to fit into the format of a treatise, is the scheme from which the wings of the Cour du Cheval Blanc were built.

In theory Serlio's schemes could date back to 1539, since that was the date when Francis I invited him to come to France, resulting in his appointment as architect to the king. Not being subordinate to the site at Fontainebleau, the schemes in Book VI may have been designed in Italy and sent to Francis I as the first contribution from his architect. Nonetheless the French-style scheme reveals such knowledge of the

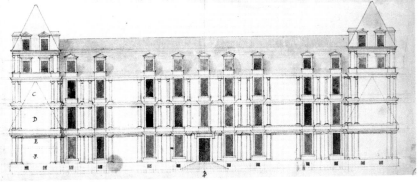

French-style scheme by Sebastiano Serlio

Taken from the manuscript of Serlio's Book VI (New York manuscript), this drawing shows
the outbuildings at the top, and at the bottom the building forming the back of the court.

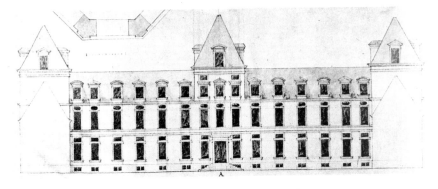

French-style scheme by Sebastiano Serlio

Drawing taken from the manuscript of Serlio's Book VI (Munich manuscript)
showing a variant for the building forming the back of the court.

architecture of the Ile de France at that period that it is unlikely to have predated
Serlio's arrival at the end of 1540 or the beginning of 1541. However pleased he may
have been to see one of his schemes chosen, he must have felt frustrated, for it is obvious
that he preferred the scheme in the Italian style, identified in the treatise as the correct
style. The Italian scheme brought into question everything done at Fontainebleau in
the last ten years. Thus Serlio had to make do with the building at the back of the
court which had already been constructed, without abandoning the idea of giving it a
new cladding, which De l'Orme and Primaticcio provided in their own way.

Moreover, Serlio's role was limited to that of a design architect. He had to be backed up by a site architect, or at least a contractor. This was not Le Breton, even though his name, transferred from the Couvent des Mathurins to the wings of the court by a sleight of hand which we have already exposed, has blotted out Serlio's. Pierre Chambiges, who was building the château of Saint-Germain at the same time, was the preferred architect, either because Le Breton was too busy, or because he proved incapable of adapting to a new style, or even because there were incipient suspicions of shortcomings and transgressions which would get him into serious trouble in De l'Orme's time[20]. Was it Chambiges who decided on mixed

*North wing of the Cour
du Cheval Blanc*

Virtually only the pilasters
and the entablature remain from
Sebastiano Serlio's building. The wing
was drastically altered in the nineteenth
century in the name of restoration.
The three original doors,
now walled over, can still be discerned,
with their pediments flattened
off level with the wall.

North wing of the Cour du Cheval Blanc. Central pavilion

The large dormer is reminiscent of the façades of Italian
churches. The chimney stacks bear the "F" of Francis I.

North wing of the Cour du Cheval Blanc

Following pages:
In the foreground, the horseshoe-shaped flight of steps.

bond, with the structural parts constructed of brick, the infilling of rendered quarry-stones, and the mouldings of the bases, the capitals and cornices of shaped brick – an unprecedented approach in France where it was traditional to use brick as infilling and dressed stone for the structure? This new way of using brick can be observed at Saint-Germain, and Serlio's drawings make no reference to the bond. However, this procedure, which is common in Italy, could have been introduced to Fontainebleau by Serlio[21].

Although it was savagely restored in the nineteenth century – the pediments over the doors were removed and the dormers reconstructed – the north wing has preserved the main features of the layout intended by Serlio. In the middle there is a pavilion with a passageway through it, and Androuet Du Cerceau's plan shows that it was designed as a sequence of lodgings. The Mathurin monks withdrew there after their monastery had been destroyed; they subsequently made way for the Secretaries of State, i.e. the king's ministers, moving into the court just behind the wing which has retained the name of Cour des Mathurins[22].

The west wing, destroyed and replaced by a railing in 1810, was similar to the north wing. It had a central pavilion forming a passageway which was to become the main entrance into the court. It probably housed the foundry where Primaticcio's bronzes based on antique models were cast, and the workshop that produced the tapestries reproducing the decoration of the Galerie François Premier. Was the south wing known as the Galerie d'Ulysse originally built as a ground floor with an attic floor, like the two other wings, in line with Serlio's scheme, and subsequently raised, with the floor containing the Galerie d'Ulysse added? Or was it originally built with this floor?

The precise date when the gallery was decorated is not known. It is only known that the painters received their first payments between 1544 and 1550, and that work was not very far advanced when Francis I died. The hypothesis of a building created in two phases, one soon after the other, and of the building being raised by one floor cannot be ruled out[23]. Nonetheless it is almost certain that the gallery floor was the work of Serlio. On both the court and the garden side a succession of bull's eye windows could be seen, a motif that had no precedent in French architecture (it became very widespread in the seventeenth century). But Serlio's work contains several examples of *occhi di bue* or *oeils-de-boeuf* included in the *finestre nei tetti*[24], i.e. a combination of the Italian oculus and the French dormer, very characteristic of the efforts Serlio made to adapt his architecture to local practices[25]. The windows in these dormers did not illuminate an attic floor, but penetrated the frieze of the tunnel vaulting in the gallery.

The written text of Book VI shows that Serlio was very familiar with the "*vasta bassecorte*" (huge bailey) of the "*ricchissimo palazzo di Fontanebleo*", and says that "*commodi loggiamenti* " (convenient lodgings) and "*botegue di mercanti* " (shopkeepers' booths) could be found there[26]. The ground-floor level of the Galerie d'Ulysse was in fact let out to "privileged traders who followed the court". The privilege accorded to these traders of being authorised – in fact forced – to follow the court on its continual travels had been renewed by Francis I on 19 March 1543[27], no doubt at the very time when they were taking possession of their brand new premises.

The three wings by Serlio, such as they were before their terrible destruction in the eighteenth and nineteenth centuries, gave the court an unusual appearance. A series of dwellings, each had its own entrance door, and most of them had a ground floor and attic floor illuminated by a dormer, a little like an estate of terraced houses. Given that the court followed a scheme designed by an Italian, the overall effect of the buildings on the court with its series of pavilions was very French. It is therefore difficult to follow the reasoning of Abbé Guilbert who found the court "Roman in style". But there is one detail that is in keeping with this view, the design of the big dormer on the north wing. Serlio has imposed the design used on the façades of the modern Italian churches of his day on the French dormer. The motif was to prove successful: it is found again as a crowning termination at the top of Rodez cathedral, the cathedral of Georges d'Armagnac, Francis I's ambassador to Venice and Rome who had helped bring about Serlio's departure for France; this crowning termination is the creation of Guillaume Philander, secretary to the bishop of Rodez, who had studied architecture in Venice with Serlio.

In the eighteenth century the south wing known as the Louis XV wing replaced the wing containing the Galerie d'Ulysse. The eastern half as far as the central pavilion was built in 1739–1740 by Jacques V Gabriel, First Architect to the King, and his son Ange-Jacques; the western half was built in 1773–1774 by Ange-Jacques Gabriel, who was then himself First Architect. It consists of a pavilion built entirely of stone, known as the Pavillon Louis XV, and a brick and stone building, with the two materials used in the traditional French way: the stone for the structure and the brick as infilling. The Gabriels intended to rebuild the whole

Cour du Cheval Blanc: Louis XV wing

Following pages:
South wing of the court, built in the eighteenth century, in place of the Galerie d'Ulysse.

court, since lodgings had to be found to satisfy a growing demand, but fortunately the financial difficulties of the reign meant that their plan came to nothing. They did not even reach the sixteenth-century pavilion where the west and south wings met, which was consequently spared. Napoleon I had to add two bays to the wing to make it reach the pavilion. It was right at the end of the Louis XV wing that Lefuel built his theatre in 1854–1856.

Androuet Du Cerceau's engravings illustrate the horse that gave the court its name and a moat that divided it in two. The horse was a plaster cast made from the mould Primaticcio had taken in Rome of Marcus Aurelius's horse on the Capitol. It was probably moulded in 1541, but never cast in bronze, and was installed on the orders of Catherine de' Medici around 1565, when the moat was being dug[28]. The horse was removed from the court in 1626 and destroyed.

The moat can be dated from Primaticcio's correspondence with Catherine de' Medici[29]. "The main part of the building was enclosed and shut off by a moat by King Charles the Ninth [...] because of the civil wars," Androuet Du Cerceau notes. The Wars of Religion led to the introduction of moats in royal châteaux, which had previously been moat-less. The medieval castle of Fontainebleau had probably been encircled by a moat, but it had disappeared. Primaticcio provided for several fixed bridges across the new moat, including one on the central axis of the court, and a drawbridge, the only crossing that would have stayed in use after the fixed bridges had been destroyed if danger threatened.

In front of the drawbridge was a gate that heralded the main entrance to the château. It may seem surprising that this did not remain in the centre, as De l'Orme had intended. The reason for the off-centre position can be understood only after entering the Cour de la Fontaine, and it was part of a total revision of De l'Orme's circulation plan. When the solution of a central entrance was adopted again at the beginning of the seventeenth century, the gateway was reused in the Cour Ovale at the Porte du Baptistère[30]. At the same time the horseshoe-shaped flight of steps was rebuilt and a parapet was constructed along the moat, the only feature still in existence today. The moat, which did not disappear until the early

Cour du Cheval Blanc: Louis XV wing

View of the central pavilion of the Louis XV wing.

nineteenth century, has had a lasting impact on the articulation of the court in which a distinction had to be made between a forecourt enclosed by wings and a court of honour running along the foot of the building at the back. The moat stopped when it reached the south wing, which was protected at the back by the Étang. Androuet Du Cerceau illustrates how the moat passed underneath the north wing in a tunnel, but in another view he shows the wing breaking off abruptly at the moat. These are probably two successive stages, the latter corresponding to the present state.

This brings into focus the important question of the link between the building at the back and the wings. The lower parts of the Pavillon des Armes and Pavillon des Poêles had been left undecorated, apparently in order to later have wings attached to them. Serlio's scheme also envisaged that the proposed wings would abut on to the building at the back. In the end the court was so wide that the wings came only to the outside corners of the pavilions. Perhaps the idea had originally been to finish the wings at this end with pavilions, as counterparts to the pavilions at the far end, adjoining the Pavillon des Armes and the Pavillon des Poêles, from corner to corner.

Between the end of the amputated north wing and the Pavillon des Armes Henri IV was able to insert a Jeu de Paume (an indoor real tennis court)[31]. It was burnt down in 1702, rebuilt identically in 1732, and is still in use today (as is the indoor court at England's Hampton Court.) This indoor court was accompanied by an open-air one. Real tennis was an extremely popular game in France: no residence of quality was without an indoor court, or even a second outdoor one. Francis I had already had one built by Le Breton on a site which has not been possible to identify[32].

⤳

The Cour du Cheval Blanc was used for tournaments and jousting contests. None took place during the reception for Emperor Charles V in December 1539, since the court did not exist then. On emerging from mass in the monastery chapel, the emperor contented himself with "touching for king's evil", imitating the kings of France who, on emerging from their coronation, demonstrated the divine origin of their power by curing those with scrofula by touching them[33]. This gesture is a reminder that the monastery was originally a hospital.

Cour du Cheval Blanc: Louis XV wing and Francis I pavilion

The failure to complete the Louis XV wing meant the pavilion
built for Francis I by Serlio was spared.

The Cour de la Fontaine, the gardens, the outlying buildings

The Cour de la Fontaine • The Jardin de Diane
The Cour des Offices, the Cour des Mathurins and the Cour des Princes •
The Jardin des Pins and the Jardin Anglais • The Grand Jardin •
The park, the waterfalls, the canal, and other outlying buildings

The creation in 1528 of the Galerie François Premier wing linking the Cour Ovale to what would become the Cour du Cheval Blanc left a space to the south between that wing and the Étang. When it was enclosed to the west by the queen-mothers' wing and the Pavillon des Poêles and to the east by the wing of the Belle-Cheminée, that space came to be known as the Cour de la Fontaine, because of a monumental fountain erected at the edge of the Étang. This court would have been completely enclosed and cut off from the Étang if a scheme to build its fourth side (1729)[1] had ever been implemented.

The proximity of a fine expanse of water attracted the Pavillon des Poêles to the side of the Étang, then in 1750–1754 Ange Jacques Gabriel built the Gros Pavillon in its place. The name is the one used by Gabriel himself, perhaps conscious of the ponderous effect created by the intrusion of the style of Versailles at Fontainebleau. The elevations of the Gros Pavillon are in fact a repetition of the elevations designed by Jules Hardouin-Mansart for Versailles, a resemblance that owes more to a line of descent than to imitation. By virtue of his position, the First Architect was responsible for heritage, and was guardian of the "grand manner" which Louis XIV's artists had perfected at Versailles. The French School having changed its site and its style, its protector, the king, ordered the destruction of some of the most outstanding works produced by that school in the sixteenth century, when it was centred at Fontainebleau.

Plate decorated with a view of the Jardin de Diane

This Sèvres porcelain plate is part of a 128-piece service created for Louis-Philippe in 1839–1844, exhibited in the Galerie des Assiettes. In the background we can see the wing containing the royal apartments and the Galerie François Premier wing.

Cour de la Fontaine

Following pages from left to right: the Louis XV wing; the Gros Pavillon; the queen-mothers' wing; the Galerie François Premier wing; the wing of the Belle Cheminée.

Cour de la Fontaine, measured drawing by Jacques Androuet Du Cerceau, 1579

From left to right: the Pavillon des Poêles with the king's study on the terrace; the queen-mothers' wing; the Galerie François Premier wing.

Cour de la Fontaine, measured drawing by Jacques Androuet Du Cerceau, 1579

View of the wing of the Belle Cheminée.

This was the fate of the Pavillon des Poêles. Androuet Du Cerceau's drawing illustrates its main façade with five bays facing the Étang; its secondary façades, with three bays, faced the Cour du Cheval Blanc and the Cour de la Fontaine. Perhaps it did not look quite as it does on the drawing when it was first built in 1530 since the cladding was renewed by Primaticcio in the 1560s.

On the first floor there was a room that Primaticcio had decorated in the 1530s, and which De l'Orme turned into a bedchamber for King Henri II (the dispersal of the decorations has already been discussed). The fireplace in the king's bedchamber prompts speculation about the purpose and whereabouts of the stoves that gave the pavilion its name. The source texts provide no answer[2]. Did the appliances heat the first floor and perhaps even the second floor from the ground-floor level? It is unlikely that they would have heated the second floor if it was already open to begin with, as a kind of belvedere with openings and no wooden frames[3]. Perhaps the stoves never worked properly or, more likely still, residents could not do without traditional fireplaces and open fires.

Running along the ground floor of the pavilion on the side facing the Étang was the Galerie Basse, covered to form a terrace. Its purpose was to provide access

Cour de la Fontaine

On this engraving by Pérelle which dates from the mid-seventeenth century we can see
from left to right: the Galerie d'Ulysse wing; the Pavillon du Billard (added in 1659);
the Pavillon des Poêles with the Galerie Basse and the king's study; the queen-mothers' wing;
the Galerie François Premier wing; the wing of the Belle Cheminée.
In the foreground the Étang, with the pavilion built in Henri IV's reign.

to the Galerie d'Ulysse wing, which touched the Pavillon des Poêles only at the
corner. The wing and the Galerie Basse must have been built at the same time.
From the Cour de la Fontaine people passed through the Galerie Basse to reach
the ground floor of the wing, and they used the terrace to go from the first floor
of the pavilion to the Galerie d'Ulysse. That did not prevent De l'Orme from
placing the small study adjoining the king's bedchamber on the terrace. It can
be seen on both Androuet Du Cerceau's and Pérelle's engravings.

Henri II never moved into his bedchamber because the wing in which the
other rooms of his apartment were to be located was not built until after his death.
The apartment was ready only in time to accommodate Catherine de' Medici. On
the death of Henri II she relinquished the queen's apartment on the Cour Ovale
to Mary Queen of Scots, the wife of the new king, Francis II. After Francis's death

Cour de la Fontaine, measured drawing
by François D'Orbay, 1676

From left to right: the wing containing
the royal apartments; the Keep; cross-section
of the Galerie François Premier wing;
wing of the Belle Cheminée.

Cour de la Fontaine, measured drawing
by François D'Orbay, 1676

Along the back, the Galerie François Premier wing;
on the left, cross-section of the queen-mothers' wing; on
the right, cross-section of the wing of
the Belle Cheminée and the Pavillon de la Porte Dorée.

The château, viewed from the Étang

On this 1738 engraving by Jacques Rigaud we see from left to right: the Étang;
the Galerie d'Ulysse wing; the Pavillon du Billard; the Pavillon des Poêles
with the Galerie Basse and the king's study.

and Mary's departure for Scotland, the queen-mother returned to the queen's apartment on the Cour Ovale. She had to vacate it yet again for the apartment on the Cour de la Fontaine after the marriage of her second son Charles IX (1570). Henri IV's widow Marie de' Medici had to make the same move after the marriage of Louis XIII, as did Anne of Austria, Louis XIII's widow, after the marriage of Louis XIV. Anne of Austria had the apartment arranged to suit her taste. The queen-mothers obviously preferred the queen's apartment to the suite of rooms that gave its name to the queen-mothers' wing, though the latter is more attractive. This is because in a royal palace the attribution of lodgings was based on hierarchy: it was better to be near the king than to be near the pond[4]. However, bringing the king and the pond closer together, though it never happened, had been on the schedule for a long time, and in creating the Galerie d'Ulysse Francis I no doubt already had the new apartment in mind. The gallery would then have taken on the role fulfilled by the first gallery for the king's apartment on the Cour Ovale, as a large, long room extending the king's bedchamber.

The contract agreed on 23 August 1558 in which De l'Orme planned the building of what became the queen-mothers' wing[5] is important in several respects. Firstly it reveals what was going to be destroyed – the wing built by Le Breton included a first-floor terrace running along its entire length at the foot of the attic storey, enabling people to go from the Galerie François Premier to the Pavillon des Poêles. Secondly, it tells us about what was to be built – the intention was for Saint-Leu stone to be used for the first time, and for the façade facing the Cour de la Fontaine to be punctuated by colossal pilasters. A colossal pilaster is a pilaster rising over a height of several floors, in this case the ground floor and the first floor. This arrangement was unknown in France at that time, and De l'Orme borrowed it from the Italians. Primaticcio, who actually built the wing, replaced this design with a façade consisting of rusticated pilasters at ground-floor level, smooth pilasters at first-floor level, and dormers with a pediment forming a broken curve. This established the order that Primaticcio and his successors used to reclad the parts previously built by Le Breton. Throughout the exterior of the château the architectural competition between Le Breton's triangular pediments and Primaticcio's – or Primaticcio-style – pediments can be observed.

The portico supporting a terrace that runs along the Galerie François Premier wing dates only from 1594. Here for the last time you can observe the system of the terraced portico, used in both the Cour Ovale and the Cour du Cheval Blanc, as a means of circulating between one block of buildings and another without going through the enfilade of rooms. Henri IV's architect has repeated Primaticcio's rusticated pilasters, but with a different rhythm. This portico replaced an earlier one built in 1570, known to us through Androuet Du Cerceau's drawing[6]. It in turn replaced a ground-floor building covered by a terrace, housing six kitchens and six pantries, constructed by Le Breton in 1534[7].

It may seem surprising that the wing housing the baths in the ground floor, the Galerie François Premier on the first floor and the king's library in the attic floor was chosen as a site for these domestic quarters, but the future Cour de la Fontaine was then no more than a service courtyard. On Androuet Du Cerceau's drawing we can clearly see the stacks of the six chimneys corresponding to the six kitchens, also providing heat for the gallery or the library, and the small side-room off the middle of the gallery with the stacks for its two fireplaces; that room was then removed to allow freedom of passage along the terrace. The decision to do away with it could not have had anything to do with the kitchens being built: they must inevitably have been deeper than the portico, so the terrace could skirt round the room.

Both in its scale and its beauty, the wing of the Belle Cheminée is an exceptional achievement in Primaticcio's work, not notable for its architectural content. The rivalry between him and De l'Orme drove Primaticcio to excel himself. Work on the wing was started in 1568, when both artists had only two years left to live.

Primaticcio, who had taken over from De l'Orme as superintendent of buildings on the death of Henri II, knew that his competitor, who had recovered the post of superintendent of the queen-mother's buildings from him, was close on his heels. He was building the Tuileries palace for the fashionable and influential Catherine de' Medici. Everything Primaticcio did in the Cour de la Fontaine had the effect of erasing the scheme De l'Orme had drawn up for Fontainebleau. The wing of the Belle Cheminée, cleverly inserted between the Galerie François Premier wing and the Pavillon de la Porte Dorée, made it possible to enlarge the king's apartment by

Gros Pavillon

This pavilion was built in 1750–1754
by Ange-Jacques Gabriel in place
of the Pavillon des Poêles.

Queen-mothers' wing

The façade of this wing was built by Primaticcio after 1559.

Galerie François Premier wing

Following pages:
The portico dates from 1594. The façade of the gallery
has been wrongly restored, with the chimneys being removed
and the dormer windows remade.

adding a guard room and a large hall in which Henri IV was to install the Belle Cheminée. By placing a large monumental staircase on the façade, the third such flight of steps in the history of the château and, like its predecessors, true to its genre with two flights, Primaticcio, in a master stroke, confirmed the proper place of the royal apartment on the Cour Ovale. De l'Orme's idea of installing the royal apartment in the Pavillon des Poêles was not only abandoned, it was slighted.

To provide access to the Cour de la Fontaine and so to the steps, Primaticcio had envisaged a passageway through the queen-mothers' wing. He had placed the drawbridge in the Cour du Cheval Blanc on the axis formed by the steps and the passageway. And to make it quite clear that the main entrance was no longer the entrance De l'Orme had created in the middle of the Cour du Cheval Blanc, he emphasised the drawbridge's importance by erecting a gateway. If he could have done so, he would no doubt have destroyed the horseshoe-shaped staircase, but De l'Orme enjoyed Charles IX's respect and the queen-mother's support. Did he have his posthumous revenge? Neglect led to the unshakable vaulting coming undone, making the ruin of the staircase inevitable, but the same fate was reserved for the staircase leading into the wing of the Belle Cheminée. Both were rebuilt in the

Wing of the Belle Cheminée

This wing was built by Primaticcio in 1568. The flight rise on the left leads
into the Salle des Gardes, the first room in the king's apartment which continues along
the Cour Ovale. The Belle Cheminée (now dismantled) gave the wing its name;
it was installed in the large first-floor room in the reign of Henri IV.

reign of Louis XIII. Nonetheless, the seventeenth century confirmed the main entrance in the central axis of the Cour du Cheval Blanc, and the eighteenth century transformed the Salle de la Belle Cheminée into a theatre: Primaticcio's staircase then became no more than a theatre staircase, a prop for a play.

The fountain which gave the court its name had been built c. 1540 by either Primaticcio or Serlio[8]. It was topped by a figure of Hercules, a youthful work by Michelangelo which Francis I had acquired. On Henri IV's orders Francine replaced that fountain with one overlooked by a figure of Perseus[9]. At the same time, in 1594, he created the Jardin de l'Étang, an artificial square island linked to the court by a footbridge. Unfortunately, the Hercules was relocated on this island and when Louis XIV had the Jardin de l'Étang destroyed to enlarge the court (1713), the statue of Hercules mysteriously disappeared[10]. Was there an apotheosis carrying him up to Olympus where the gods were assembled? Or did he fall into the water? The carp that have lived in the Étang since 1604 and whose longevity, celebrated by romantic poets, is legendary, have kept their counsel and remain proverbially dumb.

As for the figure of Perseus, it was replaced in 1827 by a mediocre statue of Ulysses by the sculptor Petitot. Offshore from the court there is a kiosk afloat on a tiny island, the Pavillon de l'Étang, built by Henri IV and rebuilt by Napoleon.

Galerie de Diane wing, measured drawing by Rodolphe Pfnor, 1863

This wing running along the east side of the Jardin de Diane was built c. 1600.

The Jardin de Diane has been known by a variety of names. In the first years of Francis I's reign when there was no other garden it was called the Jardin du Roi. After the building of a short-lived *conciergerie*, or governor's house, it was called the Jardin de la Conciergerie. In Henri II's reign it was the Jardin de la Reine, i.e. of Catherine de' Medici who did a lot to beautify it. Finally it took the name of Diana from the fountain to Diana that adorned it.

Originally the garden was bound only to the south by the buildings containing the royal apartments overlooking the Cour Ovale, and the Galerie François Premier wing. As already said, the royal apartments were doubled in depth in the reign of Charles IX. However, this did not apply to the entire length of the apartments: the window of the royal bedchamber in the Keep and a small columnar room opening directly on to the bedchamber where spared. This small room was reputedly created by Serlio and painted by Primaticcio, and is still shown on D'Orbay's 1682 drawing; apparently Louis XIV did away with it to create a

Galerie de Diane wing

The left end of the wing was created in the reign of Louis-Philippe.

Fountain of Diana

Created in 1603 by Thomas Francine,
with dogs and stags' heads by Pierre Biard.
The statue of Diana after an antique model
(1684) comes from Marly.

Egyptian door on the Pavillon des Armes

This door can be attributed
to Sebastiano Serlio.

Jardin de Diane

Wing formed by the Trinité church and the Pavillon des Armes
with the tower housing the staircase, running along
the west of the garden.

Jardin de Diane

Following pages.

second window in the royal bedchamber. As the enfilade of rooms overlooking the Jardin de Diane was considered too narrow, in 1773 the façade was moved a few feet forward from the sixteenth-century façade. The demand for larger lodgings and more of them was becoming increasingly urgent, and in 1784 the wing containing the Galerie François Premier was enlarged in its turn by the addition of an enfilade of rooms overlooking the Jardin de Diane. The most obvious effect of doubling the width of the wing in this way was the blanking out of the windows in the Galerie François Premier. The mask formed by the eighteenth-century façades counts as one of the most deplorable acts of the reigns of Louis XV and Louis XVI.

To the west the garden is enclosed by the Trinité church (its façade no more recognisable on the garden side than on the court side) and the Pavillon des Armes. It has already been suggested that this pavilion, which can be dated to the 1540s, could have been the model for the Pavillon des Poêles as it appears on Androuet Du Cerceau's drawing, after being reclad by Primaticcio. The original concept for these pavilions with an open loggia forming a belvedere could have come from Serlio, to whom the Egyptian door leading into the pavilion is attributed[11]. Serlio entitled the final pages of Book III, published in Venice in 1540 just before he left for France, "*Trattato di alcune cose maravigliose dell'Egito [...] più tosto sogni et chimere chi cose vere*" (Concerning some marvels in Egypt more like dreams and chimeras than real objects). How could Francis I, to whom the book was dedicated, have failed to ask his architect to convert these dreams into stone? Serlio was familiar with the Egyptian telamons at Tivoli, either personally or through the drawing by Peruzzi whose heir he was, and they could have served him as models[12].

Along the east side of the Jardin de Diane is a wing containing the Galerie des Cerfs on the ground, and the Galerie de Diane on the first floor. The wing, sometimes named after one gallery and sometimes the other, was built c. 1600 by one of Henri IV's architects. The court used was enclosed on the north by the Conciergerie of the château, built in 1531. It contained the lodging of the *capitaine-concierge* (governor) and the furniture repository. In Henri IV's day it was replaced by an aviary, which was remodelled into an orangery in 1647. There was a fire in the orangery in 1789, and it was demolished in 1833. The wing containing the Galerie des Chevreuils disappeared at the same time, a wing following the same design as the Galerie de Diane wing, and symmetrical to it, that joined the Pavillon des Armes to the aviary. The enclosed garden was ringed by a moat dug in 1565. Louis-Philippe turned it into a public garden, opening on to the town.

The garden's finest hours date back to the time of Catherine de' Medici who had Primaticcio's bronzes installed in it – after many tribulations, they are now

Fountain

This fountain in the apse is
on the same axis as the entrance
to the Cour des Offices.

Cour des Offices, measured drawing by Rodolphe Pfnor, 1863

Cour des Offices

Pavilion leading into the court.

Following pages:
On the right, the central apsidal pavilion
opposite the entrance.

housed in the Galerie des Cerfs. Amidst these bronze gods a figure of Diana with
a hind was enthroned, an antique marble statue given to Henri II by the Pope in
1556; now in the Louvre, this one had been replaced in 1603 by a bronze copy
made by Barthélemy Prieur in 1602. The bronze Diana was the highlight of a
fountain created by Thomas Francine, with dogs and stags' heads by the sculptor
Pierre Biard. It is this fountain that exists today, except that Prieur's Diana has
gone to join the gods in the Galerie des Cerfs; she was replaced in 1813 by a third
Diana, cast by the Kellers in 1684 and initially intended for Marly. With all her
eclipses this Diana is well and truly a goddess of the moon!

The engraving by Androuet Du Cerceau shows a curious structure in the
middle of the garden. It was a wooden trellis commissioned from Primaticcio by
Catherine de' Medici in 1560. The columns were adorned with statues of gods and
goddesses made by the most famous sculptors of the day, and now lost.

The conversion of the western servants' courtyard into a court of honour in
the early seventeenth century meant the servants' quarters had to migrate

eastwards, into the Cour des Offices, built from 1606 to 1609. It replaced buildings that can be clearly seen on Androuet Du Cerceau's drawing, identified as the Conciergerie, the Capitainerie or even the Hôtel des Ambassadeurs, all descriptions that may be used to indicate one and the same purpose. The *concierge* was not a porter, he was the governor of the château. The Conciergerie which contained lodgings was a kind of hotel: ambassadors in particular were lodged there, as etiquette did not allow them to spend the night under the same roof as the king. The building of the Cour des Offices, usually credited to the master mason Remy Collin, has to be reattributed to Gracieux Jamin[13]. The large gateway is made entirely of sandstone, while the buildings use rendered quarry stones with a brick structure: though it might have moved from one courtyard to another, the service area still wore the same livery. The large open apses that form the gateway and the middle of the main building are a motif that had been fashionable since the mid-sixteenth century; it was derived from the *nicchione* in the court of the Belvedere at the Vatican, the large apse invented by Bramante and Pirro Ligorio. The Cour des Offices, separated from the Cour Ovale by the moat, was linked to it only by a drawbridge. When the moat was filled in, the court was enclosed by a railing with an entrance gate framed by two terms by the sculptor Gilles Guérin (1640).

To the north of the Cour du Cheval Blanc, on the site the Mathurins had moved to when they were expelled from the court in 1679–1680, François d'Orbay built lodgings for the secretaries of state, or ministers, round a court which has retained the name of Cour des Mathurins. Evicted yet again, the Mathurins were given a new monastery in the town.

Banished from the Cour des Offices, the Conciergerie was established to the north of what would become the Cour des Princes. The unfortunate princes were housed in two large, austere, parallel wings hemming in a long narrow courtyard reminiscent of a barracks or a prison. This fine example of prison architecture is the work of the architects employed at Versailles, Jules Hardouin-Mansart being responsible for the westernmost wing (1701) and Jacques V Gabriel for the other wing (1738).

As well as the Jardin de Diane, the château has two other gardens: the Jardin des Pins, which was transformed into an English garden by Hurtault in 1808–1812, and the Grand Jardin, the former to the west of the Étang and the latter to its east. The Jardin des Pins merits a chapter in the history of the garden, and the Jardin Anglais is not usually mentioned, despite the fact that the first was a failure and

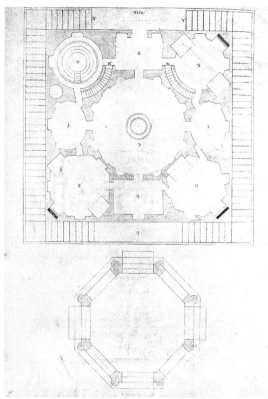

Scheme for a Pavillon des Bains by Sebastiano Serlio

This drawing is taken from Serlio's Book VI (Munich manuscript).
The pavilion which was never built would no doubt have stood in the Jardin des Pins.

Jardin des Pins

Israël Sylvestre's engraving shows the Jardin des Pins on the left, the
Pavillon de Pomone at the back and the Grotte des Pins on the right.

Grotte des Pins

The design of the Grotte des Pins is attributed
to either Primaticcio or Serlio.

the second a success. The rare and varied plants that grow in the Jardin Anglais and its English beauty no longer have the attraction of novelty, whereas the story is still told of how Francis I summoned two peasants from Gascony in 1535 to bring him seeds of the maritime pine. The idea was to recreate an Italian garden, organised round a grotto. The grotto outlived the pines, but is in a pitiful state. All that has been preserved is the façade, famous for its rustication and its atlantes, and for apparently being the first example in France of rustic architecture. The interior was decorated with rubble ornamentation consisting of pebbles and shells, and frescoes by Primaticcio.

The story of the Grotte des Pins which forms the basement floor of the west pavilion of the Galerie d'Ulysse wing, the only part of the wing to have been preserved, is intimately linked with the history of the wing and the gallery. Like the Galerie François Premier, the Galerie d'Ulysse led nowhere, or rather it led to the grotto, a pleasure grove for bucolic activities and other pastimes, protected from prying eyes by the 60 yards forming the length of the gallery. Those in the know were familiar with the little door at the end of the gallery leading down to the grotto. The grotto is attributed either to Primaticcio or to Serlio[14]. The respected opinion is that it was by Serlio, mainly because where the wing itself was concerned, the allocation of tasks to the two artists left the architecture to Serlio. Furthermore, if he did not invent rustication, Serlio at least popularised it throughout Europe; his *Libro extraordinario*, published in Lyons in 1551, provides famous examples. As for the entertainment that could be enjoyed in the Jardin des Pins, the programme was posted in the Pavillon de Pomone, a pavilion adjacent to the grotto but ten or so years older than it (1534–1535). This pavilion (destroyed in 1766) was decorated with frescoes by Rosso and Primaticcio based on the suggestive theme of the gardens of Priapus.

In his Book VI Serlio includes a scheme for a Pavillon des Bains, the only one of his schemes which he explicitly locates at the château of Fontainebleau. It would seem that this scheme was put forward in a competition which did not have any prize-winner. It is in the Jardin des Pins rather than elsewhere that this imaginary place where nymphs performed their ablutions should be located.

The Grand Jardin for its part was wide open for all to see, with the drainage canal for the Étang traversing the ground. In Francis I's day this canal was broken up into small canals cutting the plot into small square islands, and movement from one to another was effected by means of footbridges. This chequerboard garden

Jardin Anglais

This garden was created in 1808–1812 in place of the Jardin des Pins.
In the background is the Pavillon de l'Étang.

The Étang

Following pages:
The pavilion was built in Henri IV's reign,
and rebuilt in the reign of Napoleon I.

completely enclosed by walls, then known as the Jardin du Roi, was very typical of sixteenth-century French gardens. Henri IV had it re-landscaped by Claude Mollet and Thomas Francine. In the middle Francine erected a monumental fountain adorned with the Tiber, one of Primaticcio's bronze figures which gave the garden a new name. Its present state dates from 1660–1664 and it is attributed – without any proof to back it up – to André Le Nôtre.

At the north-east corner of the garden there is a building that has been called the Pavillon de Sully or the Pavillon du Chambellan, authoritatively referred to here as the Logis du Chambellan. While the mistake made in assigning the house to Henri IV's famous minister, Sully, has been corrected, people have been happy to describe a building consisting of a round tower and two pavilions as a "pavilion". For the same reasons, the Pavillon du Grand Maître becomes the Logis du Grand Maître, and the Pavillon de la Chaussée the Logis de la Chaussée. These two buildings have disappeared: one was at the south-east corner of the Grand Jardin, the other at its south-west corner, at the start of the *chaussée* or carriageway

The Fountain of the Tiber

In this drawing by Thomas Francine, engraved by Marne, we can see
the Tiber, one of the bronzes moulded after the antique by Primaticcio.
The fountain was created in 1603 and destroyed in 1664.

The Grand Jardin

A study of the Grand Jardin in its present state has not
yet been carried out. The design has been attributed to Le Nôtre, but
without any proof to back the claim.

The Étang

In the centre, the pavilion rebuilt
in Napoleon I's reign.

leading to the Porte Dorée. With the Pavillon de la Porte Dorée and the Logis du Chambellan, these two houses staked out the four corners of the Grand Jardin. This scheme, which can be seen clearly on Francine's detail drawing, has been attributed to Le Breton who was supposedly paid for the construction of the three houses in 1535. The Logis du Chambellan is unusual in appearance: its round sandstone tower and its two pavilions made of brick and rendered quarry stones create the shape of a hinge at the corner of the Grand Jardin. It seems obvious that only the round tower was built by Le Breton; it was, in fact, for the construction

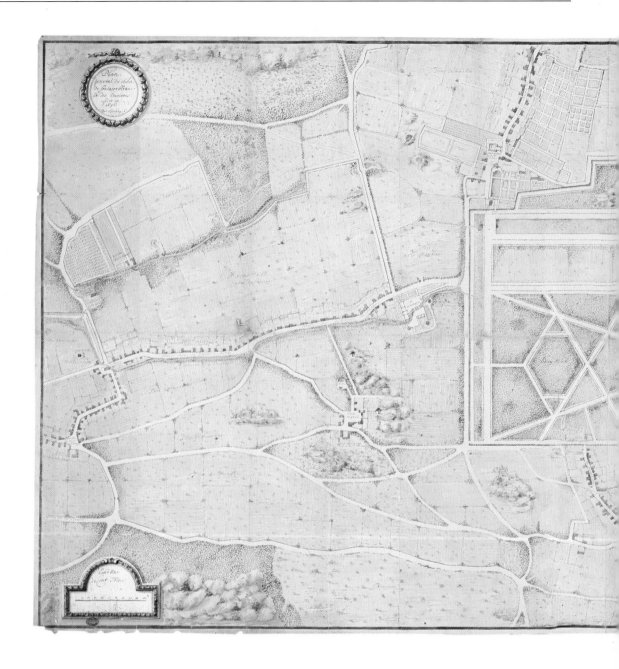

of sandstone towers that Le Breton was paid in 1535[15]. The two pavilions were added employing the same approach as used in the court by Serlio. This also applies to the two houses that have disappeared, which were likewise made up of a curious combination of round towers and pavilions. According to Abbé Guilbert[16], the kennels, next to the Logis de la Chaussée (now gone, but visible on Francine's drawing), had been built by Serlio "in the Roman style" with brick pilasters, friezes and cornices. In other words, the kennels were in the same style as the Cour du Cheval Blanc: here again, because of an obvious error in dating, the historian's evidence has not been taken seriously.

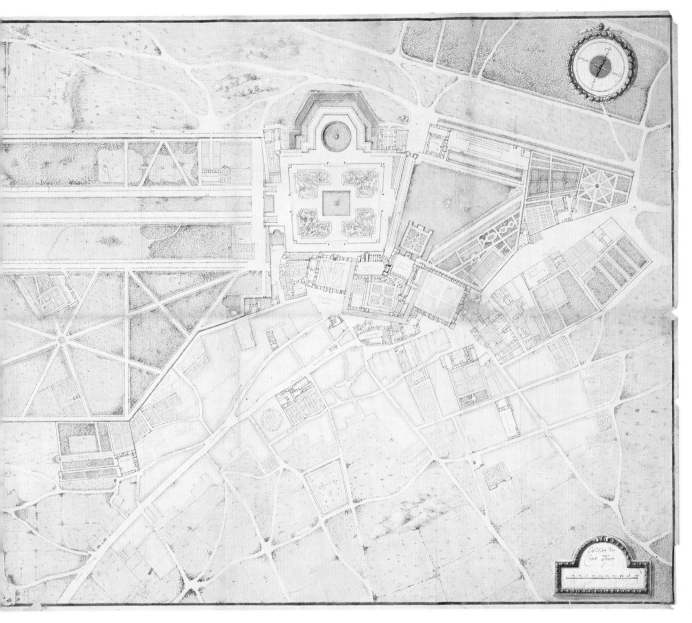

Plan of the château and its surroundings,
measured drawing by François D'Orbay, 1676 (north is at the bottom)

On the left-hand page, the boundaries of the enclosed park and the end of the canal.
On the right-hand page, above the canal, the heronry; below it, the My-Voie;
above the Grand Jardin, the Logis du Grand Maître (on the left)
and the Logis de la Chaussée or Capitainerie (on the right).
Above the Étang, the Kennels. To the right of the Cour du Cheval Blanc, the Grand Ferrare.

General view of the château of Fontainebleau

This picture by Pierre-Denis Martin the Younger,
after 1713, shows the château in its surroundings
at the end of Louis XIV's reign.

Below, a detail of the Kennels, built by Serlio in the 1540s.
We see the same architectural approach
as in the Cour du Cheval Blanc:
dormers, pilasters and brick mouldings.

Below, detail of the Capitainerie.

The Waterfalls

These form the head of the canal which only starts to the left of the road.
On the right, the Grand Jardin.

A royal château is not restricted within the confines of its buildings and gardens. An enclosed hunting park was created by means of several purchases, made from the time of Francis I to that of Henri IV. In 1608–1609 Henri IV had a canal, measuring one and a half kilometres long, constructed across the park. To head the canal waterfalls were introduced at the bottom of the Grand Jardin (1661–1662). Among other features worth mentioning are the heronry, the stables, the My-Voie (Halfway House) that Catherine de' Medici had built, and the town itself. In the sixteenth century prelates and great lords built mansions there, living in them only when the king was in residence. But there is little left, except for the Portail du Grand Ferrare, leading into the mansion of Hippolyte d'Este, Cardinal of Ferrara, facing the entrance into the château, the only work by Serlio at Fontainebleau which has never been contested. It was said that if Serlio had built within the château, he would have said so in his treatise. But what was there to boast about?

Canal overflow

At the eastern end of the canal.

The Canal

Following pages.

Building a servants' courtyard? For a great architect, his involvement amounted to failure. The château resisted any attempt to impose order on its natural tendency to proliferate. What De l'Orme attempted to do, Primaticcio undid. Louis XIV's architects, who demonstrated at Versailles how town and country could be subjegated to the king, were modest in their undertakings at Fontainebleau. If they had attempted a grand gesture, it would have clashed with something. The gardens remain sixteenth-century gardens, set beside the château, not an integral part of it. The canal is not part of any composition, and Gabriel's design came to nothing.

There is no reason to complain, however. What is to be gained by having a second Chambord or a second Versailles? At Fontainebleau there is a surprise around every corner, the sketch of an idea that the imagination can seize upon. Fontainebleau's destiny was written in the egg, in that oval château which Francis I chose to adapt rather than destroy.

Notes

CHAPTER I
Pages 10 to 33

1. Given as 1527 in the text, but 1528 in the new style. In the sixteenth century, the year started at Easter, and the months of January and February, and part of March, were the last months of the year. To bring the start of the year back to 1 January, historians usually postdate the dates in question, placing the note "new style", abbreviated to "n. st.", after them.
2. *Négociations diplomatiques de la France avec la Toscane*, 1859–1886, vol. II, p. 17.
3. *La vie de Benvenuto Cellini écrite by lui-même* (first published 1728), French translation by Nadine Blamoutier, Paris, 1986, p. 260.
4. According to Antoine de Saint-Yon, *Ordonnances des eaux et forêts*, 1610.
5. Letters of December 1529, quoted by Abbé Guilbert, *Description du château, bourg et forêt de Fontainebleau*, 1731, p. 262.
6. *Comptes des bâtiments du rois (1528–1571)*, Paris, 1877–1880, vol. I, p. 59 ff. In the notes below the work will be mentioned under the abbreviated title: *Comptes...*
7. Ibid., pp. 25–50.
8. Ibid., p. 32.
9. For the Le Breton family, see Henri Stein, "La famille de l'architecte Gilles Le Breton", in *Annales de la Société historique et archéologique du Gâtinais*, vol. 27 (1909), pp. 169–183.
10. Félix Herbet, "Les architectes …"
11. *Comptes...*, vol. I, op. cit., p. 59.
12. Ibid., p. 119. It does seem that until his death in 1531 Champverne himself was the only officially accredited controller. Nevertheless, Pierre Paule and Des Hôtels are mentioned in a document of 28 August 1528 as having carried out an inspection in the presence of Champverne (*Comptes...*, op. cit. vol. I, p. 59). They apparently carried out the job before holding the official post.
13. Copy of the inscription in the *Revue universelle des Arts*, vol. I, 1855, p. 211, with an obvious error

regarding the date of death (28 December 1637).
14. On Cognac, we have consulted "Cognac: Cité marchande", 1989, published by the Inventaire général in the collection *Cahiers du Patrimoine*; on Moulins, the large *Histoire de Moulins* by Henry Faure, Moulins, 1900. P. Pradel in "Le premier édifice de la Renaissance en France", *Mémoires des Antiquaires de France*, 1969, p. 234, mentions a joiner called Pierre Napolitain at Moulins. There was a Marsault Paule, sculptor, active in Berry at the beginning of the sixteenth century: cf. *Guide du Patrimoine – Région Centre*, 1988, p. 228. Linking him with St. Francis of Paola, born at Paola in Calabria and summoned to Plessis-lès-Tours in 1480 by Louis XI, is no doubt more hazardous, but perhaps not devoid of interest. We will pass over the meeting between Louise of Savoy and the saint, who supposedly foretold that she would be the mother of a king. But Francis of Paola was a Franciscan, and the Ave Maria-monastery where Pierre Paule arranged to be buried was a Franciscan institution founded by Louis XI in 1480: perhaps this is a coincidence.
15. Jean-Pierre Babelon, *Nouvelle Histoire de Paris. Paris au XVIe siècle*, 1986, p. 58.
16. Account of the reign of Emperor Charles V, 1539, quoted in *Guide du Patrimoine – Ile-de-France*, p. 272.
17. For the conditions and dates of Serlio's time in France, see William B. Dinsmoor, "The literary remains of Sebastian Serlio", *The Art Bulletin*, 1942, pp. 55–74.
18. *Comptes...*, op. cit., vol. I, p. 171.
19. Ibid., p. 267.
20. Ibid., p. 267.
21. Ibid., p. 286.
22. Maurice Roy, *Artistes et monuments de la Renaissance en France*, 2 vols, 1929–1934, vol. I, p. 147.

CHAPTER II
Pages 34 to 53

1. *La Vie de Cellini...*, op. cit., p. 260.

2. Francis A. Yates, *The Valois Tapestries*, London 1959, pp. 53–54.
3. Sebastiano Serlio, *Book VII*, Frankfurt, 1575, p. 97.
4. Philibert De l'Orme, *Premier Tome de l'architecture*, 1567, fol. 202 v.
5. *Comptes...*, op. cit., vol. I, p. 165.
6. Cf. Bertrand Jestaz, "Étiquettes et distributions intérieures dans les maisons royales de la Renaissance", *Bulletin monumental*, 1988, pp. 109–120.
7. Quoted by Louis Hautecœur, *Histoire de l'architecture classique en France*, vol. I² (1965), p. 97. The reference given by Hautecœur for this quotation is wrong.
8. Félix Herbet, *Le château de Fontainebleau*, Paris, 1937, p. 351.
9. Abbé Guilbert, op. cit., vol. I, p. 12.
10. Jean-Pierre Babelon, *Demeures parisiennes sous Henri IV et Louis XIII* (1965), new edition 1991, p. 260.
11. Édouard Jacques Ciprut, *Mathieu Jacquet, sculpteur d'Henri IV*, 1967.

CHAPTER III
Pages 54 to 93

1. The tapestries are at the Kunsthistorisches Museum in Vienna. For information on them, see Henri Zerner, *L'Art de la Renaissance*, 1996, pp. 86–87. The publication of a 1540 document by C. Grodecki ("Sur les ateliers de Fontainebleau") leaves no doubt regarding the date when the set of tapestries was commissioned. The date when it was completed, on the other hand, is not known.
2. William McAllister-Johnson, "On some neglected usages of Renaissance, diplomatic correspondence", *Gazette des Beaux-Arts*, January 1972, pp. 5–54.
3. Quoted in H. Zerner, op. cit., p. 84. The way the argument is developed below is entirely drawn from this author's commentary on the gallery which has shed a completely new light on it.
4. Sylvie Béguin, "New Evidence for Rosso in France", *The Burlington

Magazine, December 1989, pp. 828–838.
5. As details of these changes are only of moderate interest to the reader, we are giving them as a note. On the west wall, the low side doors were replaced in 1639 by a high central door leading into the vestibule. At the west end of the north wall a new door was made in 1688 leading on to the large staircase that had just been created; when this was done the stucco work had to be remade in the sixteenth-century manner to frame the new door. On the east side, the height of the side doors (one is a false door) was raised and the decoration redone by Gabriel in 1757. At the east end of the south wall a concealed door was inserted in the days of Louis-Philippe.
6. It has been said that the side-room had to go because of the building of the kitchens, completed in 1535; they were the first low-level addition running along the wing, with the roof forming a terrace. As the room is still featured on Androuet Du Cerceau's measured drawing (p. 135), it was assumed that an entrance has been made on either side of the room to enable people to move along the terrace. But the kitchens were so wide that the terrace must have passed round the side-room. The problem arose only when the kitchens were replaced by a portico, which was too narrow to allow circulation along the terrace without getting rid of the room. The portico was built by Primaticcio in 1565 at the same time as the wing of the Belle Cheminée. That is when the side-room was destroyed, just after being drawn by Androuet Du Cerceau.
7. It had been noticed that the wainscot on the south dated partly from the nineteenth century: this is why. The number of fireplaces grew. The 1528 specification (*Comptes...*, op. cit., vol. I., p. 45) envisaged five fireplaces for the gallery and the side-rooms. On Androuet Du Cerceau's drawing, there are: six fireplaces on the south wall of the gallery, one on each pier; two in the south side-room

and one in the north side-room.

8. Jean Guillaume, "La galerie dans le château français: place et fonction"', in *Revue de l'art*, no. 102, 1993, pp. 32–42.

9. Abbé Guilbert, op. cit., vol. II, p. 15.

10. See J. Guillaume's article in Sylvie Béguin, *La galerie d'Ulysse*, 1985.

11. Maurice Roy, *Artistes...*, op. cit., vol. I, pp. 262–264.

12. Pierre-Jean Mariette, *Abecedario et autres notes inédites* (published posthumously), vol. IV (1857–1858), p. 212.

13. Abbé Guilbert, op. cit., vol. II, p. 14.

14. Library of the Institut de France, manuscript 1014.

15. Library of the Institut de France, manuscript 1016.

CHAPTER IV

Pages 94 to 129

1. Abbé Guilbert, op. cit., vol. II, p. 3.

2. Ibid., p. 50.

3. Jean-Jacques Rousseau, *Les Confessions*, Book VIII, 1765–1770.

4. Abbé Guilbert, op. cit., vol. II, pp. 27 and 28.

5. Quoted by Félix Herbet, *Le Château...*, op. cit., pp. 65–66, no reference given.

6. Pierre-Jean Mariette, marginal note in "Peintures de l'Institution de Bologne", 1759, in *Abecedario*, op. cit., vol. VI (1859), p. 293 ff.

7. Félix Herbet, *Le Château...*, op. cit., pp. 376–377, gives two contradictory accounts of the decoration of this room. This is because he has confused the Cabinet du Roi, which was decorated in Henri IV's reign and became the Salle du Conseil, with the room on the column that opened directly on to the bedchamber in the Keep which still appears on D'Orbay's 1676 measured drawing. It was the latter room that was decorated with paintings by Primaticcio. It is believed to have been removed in Louis XIV's reign.

CHAPTER V

Pages 132 to 163

1. *La Vie de Cellini*, op. cit., p. 260.

2. The contract of 5 August 1531 for building the external flight of steps is known only through the allusion to it in the contract of 10 March 1541 (n. st.) regarding the building of the staircase: cf. *Comptes...*, op. cit., vol. I, p. 210.

3. Abbé Guilbert, op. cit., p. 19.

4. The description just given of the layout of the royal apartments and how they worked is taken entirely from the remarkable study by Françoise Boudon and Monique Chatenet, "Les logis du roi de France". Our only reservation relates to the reconstruction of the sixteenth-century staircase; if we go by Du Cerceau's plan, it was made up of just two parallel flight rises, one for the queen and the other for the royal children. It is probable that there was a second, single, central flight rise, but there is no evidence of this. It is impossible to go to the seventeenth and eighteenth-century plans for corroboration because of the way the staircase was swung round at the beginning of the seventeenth century. If it did have two flights (a first double flight with two parallel flight rises and a second central flight), the staircase would have been even more monumental than the external steps, even though it did not lead to the king. Moreover, in 1556, according to Gaspar de Vega quoted by the authors (note 31), "nowhere in the palace would one find a good staircase".

5. The argument about to be developed is taken from the article by L. Châtelet-Lange, "La forma ovale si come costumarono li antichi romani: salles et cours ovales en France au seizième siècle", *Architectura*, 1976, pp. 128–147. Only two lines of argument are missing from this remarkable article, which would in fact have supported its conclusions. Believing the Salle du Guet to have been destroyed in 1601, the author has not located the christening of Louis XIII in it, so has failed to make the connection with the engraving by Jean Le Clerc and Léonard Gaultier, which is so conclusive. Nor has the author quoted Serlio's loggia scheme, consistently placed on the site of the Salle de Bal wing, and wrongly so in our view.

6. The plan by Androuet Du Cerceau could lead us to doubt whether the building really was rectangular. We attribute the fact that the rectangular envelope is not shown right round the circumference to a draughtsman's oversight.

7. *Comptes...*, op. cit., vol. I, p. 39. The room was to occupy the whole ground floor, which had only an attic storey above it. It really is the room that can be seen on Androuet Du Cerceau's drawing.

8. L. Châtelet-Lange cites a very significant passage by Sauval on the use of the Salle du Guet at the Louvre.

9. Father Dan, in *Le Trésor des merveilles de la Maison royale de Fontainebleau*, 1642, p. 278, gives a long description of the christening ceremony of the future Louis XIII. There were in fact temporary structures in the actual court, including a "bridge" crossing the court from west to east, enabling the king to come out of the royal bedchamber in the Keep and go straight to the platform in the Salle du Guet without ever going down. From Father Dan's description, we recognise the room depicted in the engraving by Le Clerc and Gaultier: in a "big place [...] surrounded by balustrades, there was a table covered by a canopy [...] intended to receive Monseigneur le Dauphin".

10. Serlio is the person mainly responsible for this confusion, due to the fact that the scheme for the Salle de Bal was in competition with his own. One passage in Serlio's treatise gives us some clue regarding the confusion. Serlio in fact locates his scheme between the "appartamenti di Principi" and "una capella". Now the Salle de Bal lies between the Pavillon de la Porte Dorée and Saint-Saturnin chapel: it is not adjacent to the royal apartments, far less to those of the "principi", i.e. the royal children. In fact in the same text the expression "camere reali" is used to refer to the royal apartments – whereas the Salle du Guet actually was between the Pavillon des Enfants royaux and Saint-Saturnin chapel.

11. This date itself is only an indication since more work was carried out on the roof timbers after the death of Francis I.

12. F. Herbet in *Le Château...*, op. cit., pp. 326–327, doubted whether the wing envisaged in the 1528 specification had really been built, for he would not allow himself to recognise it in the small view. He refused to identify the upstairs gallery on it, seeing only an attic storey. However, the importance accorded to the dormers leaves no doubt as to the "noble" use of that attic storey.

13. Contract with the carpenter Claude Girard, published by F. Herbet in *Le Château*, op. cit., p. 329. In our view, the payment made to the mason Pierre Girard at some unspecified date between 1541 and 1550 (*Comptes...*, op. cit., vol. I p. 209) really relates to the Salle de Bal wing, as Herbet thought, and not to the Salle du Guet, as L. Châtelet-Lange believes (op. cit., p. 139 and note 42). In describing this payment, the copyist of the accounts has written Val instead of Bal.

14. This ground floor area is now known as the Salle des Colonnes, due to the columns that were added at the time of Louis-Philippe's restorations to support the floor of the Salle de Bal. We do not feel that there was ever any intention of placing Primaticcio's copies of antiquities there; that suggestion is linked to Serlio's loggia scheme which, as we have seen, was located on the site of the Salle du Guet and not on that of the Salle de Bal.

CHAPTER VI

Pages 164 to 193

1. Letters patent of December 1529, quoted by F. Herbet, *Le Château...*, op. cit., p. 5.

2. *Comptes...*, op. cit., vol. I, p. 59. What is written there is "5 June 1529", not "5 June 1528"; we felt that date had to be corrected since the approval of the work took place in 1528.

3. Ibid., p. 48.

4. Ibid., p. 66.

5. Ibid., p. 134.

6. Father Dan, op. cit., p. 128. See also Jean-Marie Pérouse de Montclos, *L'Architecture à la française*, 1982, p. 74.

7. *Comptes...*, op. cit., vol. II, p. 362.

8. *Comptes...*, op. cit., vol. I, pp. 189, 191, 201, 202, 204.

9. F. Herbet, *Le Château....*, op. cit., p. 74.

10. In his reconstruction, *Les origines de Fontainebleau*, A. Bray places the church north of the cloister, with no archaeological justification. He asked no questions regarding the significance of the three arches. We site the church and the open court of the cloister in the space lying between the Pavillon des Poêles and the Pavillon des Orgues, a confined space admittedly, but it should be remembered that we are talking about a small community of a few monks. Some writers attribute these three Renaissance arches to the church; but there is no mention in the written records of the church being rebuilt, so until it was demolished it must have retained its thirteenth-century architecture.

11. Herbet believed that the side chapels had been added by Primaticcio during Charles IX's reign, but De l'Orme decorated them in 1554.

12. M. Roy, *Artistes...*, op. cit., vol. I, p. 251. The same specification refers to roofing over the Pavillon des Orgues, which has led people to conclude that it was contemporary with the church. We have tried to explain why it must have been earlier.

13. Ibid., p. 252.

14. Ibid., p. 275.

15. F. Herbet, *Le Château...*, op. cit., p. 90, contract of 19 March 1632. For a long time this reconstruction was attributed to Le Mercier.

16. Bringing the first storey of the façade forward between the Unnamed Pavilion and the Pavillon des Poêles meant the terrace was covered over, to become the Galerie des Assiettes. The middle aisle of the church with its rectangular windows (preserved) was masked by a wall with round-headed windows; the terrace was replaced by a roof; the ground-floor wall was brought forward, so removing both the arrangement installed by Henri IV and the projecting line of the pavilions.

17. Father Dan, op. cit., pp. 30 and 33; Abbé Guilbert, op. cit., vol. II, p. 43.

18. Léon Palustre, *La Renaissance en France*, 3 vols, 1879–1885, vol. I, p. 173.

19. Jean Guillaume in *Serlio* has given a very subtle analysis of the "Frenchness" of Serlio's architectural vocabulary.

20. Although Chambiges is mentioned in *Comptes...*, op. cit., vol. I, p. 154, as being active at Fontainebleau, he has disappeared from the history of the château because there was a seeming contradiction between the dates when he was present (between 1538 and 1546) and those of the buildings on the Cour du Cheval Blanc that could be attributed to him.

21. According to the *Comptes...*, Le Breton used brick for the dividing walls, the fireplaces and the chimney stacks only.

22. The Mathurins' presence in this wing has contributed greatly to the confusion between it and the building work carried out at the monastery in 1528.

23. The carpentry contract of 7 September 1527 (*Comptes...*, op. cit., vol. I, p. 66) relates to the Couvent des Mathurins, not the Galerie d'Ulysse wing as Herbet claimed.

24. Serlio, Book VII, pp. 80, 83, 195.

25. For this question and the line of argument that follows, we make use of J. Guillaume's comments in S. Béguin, *La galerie d'Ulysse*, op. cit.

26. Serlio, Munich manuscript, fol. 31 v.

27. F. Herbet, *Le Château...*, op. cit., p. 50.

28. Abbé Guilbert, op. cit., vol. II, p. 43.

29. Henri Stein, "Quelques lettres inédites de Primatice", *Annales du Gâtinais*, 1910, pp. 307–325.

30. F. Herbet, *Le Château...*, op. cit., pp. 9 and 10.

31. Ibid., p. 23.

32. Ibid., p. 24.

33. Ibid., p. 16.

CHAPTER VII
Pages 194 to 235

1. François Fossier, *Les dessins du fonds Robert de Cotte à la Bibliothèque nationale de France*, Paris-Rome, 1997, pp. 438–442.

2. Depending on which part of *Comptes...* one reads, the stoves were on the first floor (op. cit., vol. I, p. 204) or the ground floor (ibid., p. 371).

3. This observation results from consulting Androuet Du Cerceau's measured drawing. On Pérelle's engravings, the openings have visibly been fitted with joinery work.

4. Cf. Monique Chatenet, "Une demeure royale au milieu du XVIᵉ siècle. La distribution des espaces au château de Saint-Germain-en-Laye", *Revue de l'art*, no. 81, 1988, pp. 20–30.

5. M. Roy, *Artistes...*, op. cit., vol. I, p. 275.

6. On the small painted view in the Galerie François Premier (p. 145), it is the kitchens that can be seen.

7. *Comptes...*, op. cit., vol. I, p. 58: contract of 14 April 1534, approval on 13 November 1534, payment on 18 February 1535 (n. st.); ibid., p. 78, contract, approval and payment for carpentry work on the same piece of work.

8. In most studies, Primaticcio is credited with the fountain. Louis Hautecœur, op. cit., vol. I² (1965), p. 120, attributes it to Serlio, with no reference, but as if it was an incontrovertible fact.

9. This Perseus, which had the heel-wings of Mercury, has been taken for a Mercury (Abbé Guilbert, op. cit., vol. I, p. 38).

10. Liliane Châtelet-Lange, "Michelangelo's Hercules in Fontainebleau", Pantheon, vol. XXX (1972), pp. 455–468.

11. This link is taken from J. Guillaume's article, "Fontainebleau 1530", op. cit. The telamones are now in the Vatican museum.

12. Jean-Pierre Babelon, *Demeures parisiennes...*, op. cit., p. 260.

13. This line of argument is inspired by J. Guillaume's article in S. Béguin, *La galerie d'Ulysse*, op. cit., in which the author demonstrates that the implantation of the gardens governed the development of the buildings.

14. The name of Antoine Jacquet known as Grenoble has been found in the 1541–1550 accounts (*Comptes...*, op. cit., vol. I, p. 202) as sculptor of the atlantes. This reading of the text does not seem to be decisive.

15. *Comptes...*, op. cit., vol. I, p. 62. Payment to Le Breton in 1534 for masonry work carried out "on the tower built anew at the corner of the Grand Jardin [...] near the kennels". The work was approved by Pierre Paule on 27 March 1532. The payment includes supplying the materials, a list of which is appended. There is no mention of bricks.

- Ibid., p. 63. Payment to Le Breton in 1534 for masonry work on the "rebuilt" kennels. Approved by Pierre Paule on 10 November 1534. No bricks are mentioned in the list of materials.

- Ibid., p. 65. Payment to Le Breton in 1534 for new masonry "in the two towers and buildings" on the Grand Jardin "both on the Entragues side [south-east corner] and the Hôtel de Vendosme side [north-east corner, see Herbet, *Le Château...*, p. 453, note 2]". Approved by Pierre Paule on 13 November 1534. No bricks are mentioned in the list of materials.

16. Abbé Guilbert, op. cit., vol. II, p. 102.

Chronology

1137

Charters issued by Louis VII signed at Fontainebleau, proving the existence of a royal residence there.

1169

Consecration of Saint-Saturnin chapel by Thomas à Becket, Archbishop of Canterbury, in exile in France.

1259

Foundation of a Trinitarian monastery (known as the Couvent des Mathurins) by Louis IX (St Louis).

1431

Letter from the Dauphin (subsequently Charles VII) to his mother Isabeau of Bavaria, testifying to recent work at the residence of Fontainebleau.

1519

Death of Leonardo da Vinci.

1525

Battle of Pavia. Francis I taken prisoner by Emperor Charles V.

1527

• Return of Francis I from captivity (17 March). Entry into Paris (14 April).
• Sack of Rome by Emperor Charles V's troops (May).
• Work on the Couvent des Mathurins in anticipation of the king's arrival at Fontainebleau (August).

1528

• Letter from Francis I to the Paris city council informing them of his intention to make Paris or the surrounding area his usual place of residence (15 March).
• Specification of work to be carried out at the château of Fontainebleau and the Couvent des Mathurins, signed Gilles Le Breton (28 April).

1530

Arrival of Rosso in France.

1531

Death of Louise of Savoy, mother of Francis I (22 September).

1532

Arrival of Primaticcio in France.

1533

Start of decorative work in the king's bedchamber in the Keep by Primaticcio.

1535

• C. 1535, start of decorative work in the Galerie François Premier by Rosso.
• Death of Pierre Paule, known as The Italian, architect to the king, worked at Fontainebleau (28 December).

1539

Visit by Emperor Charles V to Fontainebleau (24–30 December).

1540

• Primaticcio sent to Rome to acquire antiquities, and make moulds of the most famous antique statues (February).
• Edict of Fontainebleau promoting the repression of heresy (1 June).
• Death of Rosso (14 November).
• Arrival of Cellini at Fontainebleau.
• Publication in Venice of *Le antiquità di Roma* by Serlio, dedicated to Francis I.
• Arrival of Serlio at Fontainebleau (end of year or beginning of following year).

1541

• Start of decorative work in the bedchamber of the Duchess of Étampes by Primaticcio.
• Start of work by Serlio on the Cour du Cheval blanc.
• Arrival of Vignola at Fontainebleau.

1542

Start of Cellini's work for the Porte Dorée.

1543

Return of Vignola to Italy.

1544

Christening at Fontainebleau of Francis, son of the Dauphin Henri and subsequently Francis II (10 February).

1545

Return of Cellini to Italy.

1546

• C. 1546, start of decorative work in the Galerie d'Ulysse and perhaps in the Salle de Bal.
• Start of reconstruction of the Louvre by Lescot.

1547

• Death of Francis I. Accession of Henri II (31 March).
• De l'Orme, Architect to the King. Serlio leaves Fontainebleau for Lyons.

1552

Arrival in France of Nicolò dell'Abate.

1554

Death of Serlio.

1559

Death of Henri II. Accession of Francis II (10 July).

1560

• The Assemblée des nobles meeting at Fontainebleau (21–31 August) decides to convene the États généraux.
• Death of Francis II. Accession of Charles IX (5 December).

1562

Massacre of Wassy (1 March). Start of the Wars of Religion.

1564

Start of work on the wing known as the wing of the Belle Cheminée.

1570

• Death of De l'Orme (8 January).
• Death of Primaticcio.

1572

Massacre of the Protestants on Saint-Bartholomew's Day (24 August).

1574

Death of Charles IX. Accession of Henri III (30 May).

1579

Publication of the volume entitled *Les Plus Excellents Bastiments de France* by Jacques Androuet Du Cerceau, containing measured drawings of the château.

1589

Death of Henri III. Accession of Henri IV (2 August).

1593

Entry of Henri IV into Paris (22 March).

1597

Start of work on the Belle Cheminée by Mathieu Jacquet.

1598

• Edict of Nantes setting out the freedoms accorded to the Protestants (13 April).
• Arrival in France of Thomas and Alexandre Francine.

1601

C. 1601, start of decorative work in the first Galerie de Diane, by Ambroise Dubois.

1602

• Death of Toussaint Dubreuil, Painter to the King.
• Martin Fréminet appointed to replace Dubreuil.

1605

Start of decorative work on the Cabinet Ovale, with the story of Theagenes and Chariclea, painted by Ambroise Dubois.

1606
Christening at Fontainebleau of the Dauphin, subsequently Louis XIII, and his two sisters (14 September).

1607
C. 1607, construction of the Porte du Baptistère.

1608
• Start of decorative work in the Trinité church by Fréminet.
• Digging of the canal.

1609
Contract for the building of the Cour des Offices, signed by Remy Collin.

1610
Death of Henri IV. Accession of Louis XIII (14 May)

1619
Death of Fréminet.

1642
Publication of *Le Trésor des Merveilles de la maison royale de Fontainebleau*, by Father Dan.

1643
Death of Louis XIII. Accession of Louis XIV (14 May). Regency of Anne of Austria.

1648–1652
The Fronde (civil war).

1660
Marriage of Louis XIV.

1661
• Start of Louis XIV's personal rule.
• Creation of the waterfalls at the head of the canal.

1672
Louis XIV takes up residence at Versailles.

1679
Construction of the Cour des Mathurins with houses for the secretaries of state.

1685
Revocation of the Edict of Nantes by the Edict of Fontainebleau (17 October).

1715
Death of Louis XIV. Accession of Louis XV (1 September). Regency of the Duke of Orleans.

1723
Louis XV attains his majority.

1739
Start of building work on the Louis XV wing on the Cour du Cheval blanc.

1750
Start of construction of the Gros Pavillon by A.J. Gabriel.

1751
Start of decorative work in the Salle du Conseil.

1752
Performance of *Le Devin du village* by Jean-Jacques Rousseau at Fontainebleau.

1762
Start of work by A. J. Gabriel on the Petit Trianon at Versailles.

1774
Death of Louis XV. Accession of Louis XVI (10 May).

1784
Doubling of depth of the Galerie François Premier wing on the Jardin de Diane side.

1786
Decorative work by the architect Pierre Rousseau in the queen's apartment.

1789
Fall of the Bastille (14 July).

1793
Execution of Louis XVI (21 January).

1799
Coup d'état of 18 Brumaire (23 January).

1803
Construction of the Manège by Maximilien-Joseph Hurtault.

1804
• Visit by Pope Pius VII to Fontainebleau (24–28 November).
• Coronation of Napoleon (2 December)

1808
Transfer of École spéciale militaire from Fontainebleau to Saint-Cyr.

1810
• Start of decorative work in the second Galerie de Diane.
• Start of work on the Jardin Anglais by Hurtault.

1812
Pope Pius VII detained under guard at Fontainebleau (19 June).

1813
Concordat of Fontainebleau (25 January).

1814
• Departure of Pope Pius VII from Fontainebleau (23 January).
• Abdication of Napoleon I (6 April) and his farewell to the Guard (20 April).

1815
Treaty of Paris. End of the Empire. Second restoration of Louis XVIII.

1824
Death of Louis XVIII. Accession of Charles X (16 September).

1830
Abdication of Charles X (9 August). Accession of Louis-Philippe.

1848
Downfall of Louis-Philippe (24 February). Proclamation of the Republic (17 March).

1851
Coup d'état by Louis-Napoleon (2 December).

1852
Reinstatement of the Empire (2 December).

1854
Construction of the theatre by Hector Lefuel.

1870
Collapse of the Empire.

1979
Creation of the Musée Napoléon with the donation from Prince Napoléon and the Comtesse de Witt

Bibliography

Unless otherwise specified, the place of publication is Paris

ANDROUET DU CERCEAU, Jacques, *Les Plus Excellents Bastiments de France*, vol. II, 1579.

BÉGUIN, Sylvie, CHASTEL, André, PRESSOUYRE, Sylvia and ZERNER, Henri, "La galerie de François Ier à Fontainebleau", special number of *Revue de l'art*, 1972.

BÉGUIN, Sylvie, GUILLAUME, Jean and ROY, Alain, *La Galerie d'Ulysse à Fontainebleau*, 1985.

BÉGUIN, Sylvie, "Two notes on decoration in the Galerie François Ier at Fontainebleau", *Journal of the Warburg and Courtauld Institutes*, vol. LVII (1994), pp. 270–278.

BOTTINEAU, Yves, *L'Art d'Ange-Jacques Gabriel à Fontainebleau*, 1962.

BOUDON, Françoise and CHATENET, Monique, "Les logis du roi de France au XVIe siècle", *Architecture et vie sociale à la Renaissance*, papers from the colloquium held at Tours, Centre d'études supérieures de la Renaissance, 6–10 June 1988, studies collected by J. Guillaume, 1994, pp. 65–82.

BRAY, Albert,
"Les origines de Fontainebleau avant François Ier", *Bulletin monumental*, 1935, pp. 171–214.
– "Le premier grand escalier du château de Fontainebleau et les anciens escaliers de la cour Ovale", *Bulletin monumental*, 1940, pp. 192–203.

CHASTEL, André, "L'escalier de la cour Ovale à Fontainebleau", *Essays in the History of Architecture presented to R. Wittkower*, 1967, pp. 74–80.

CHÂTELET-LANGE, Liliane, "Michelangelo's Hercules in Fontainebleau", *Pantheon*, vol. XXX (1972), pp. 455–468.

Comptes des bâtiments du Roi (1528-1571), published by Léon de LABORDE, 1877–1880.

DAN, Father Pierre, *Le Trésor des Merveilles de la Maison royale de Fontainebleau*, 1642.

Galerie de la Reine dite de Diane à Fontainebleau, published by Jacques-Édouard Gatteaux and Louis-Pierre Baltard, after the drawings of L.-P. Baltard and C. Percier, 1858.

DIMIER, Louis, *Les Grands Palais de François Ier: Fontainebleau, publié sous la direction de Louis Dimier*, 1910.

GEBELIN, François, *Les Châteaux de la Renaissance*, 1927.

GRODECKI, Catherine, "Sur les ateliers de Fontainebleau sous François Ier", *Bulletin de la Société de l'histoire de Paris et de l'Île-de-France*, 1976 –1977, p. 215.

GUILBERT, Abbé Pierre, *Description historique du château, bourg et forest de Fontainebleau*, 2 vols, 1731.

GUILLAUME, Jean and GRODECKI, Catherine, "Le jardin des Pins à Fontainebleau", *Bulletin de la Société de l'histoire de l'art français*, 1978, pp. 43–51.

GUILLAUME, Jean, "Fontainebleau 1530: le pavillon des Armes et sa porte égyptienne', *Bulletin monumental*, 1979, pp. 225–240.

– "Serlio et l'architecture française", *Sebastiano Serlio*, papers of the history of architecture seminar, Vicenza, 1987, pp. 67–78.

HERBET, Félix, "Les architectes du château de Fontainebleau", *Brie et Gâtinais*, February 1910, pp. 1–16.
– *L'Ancien Fontainebleau*, 1912.
– *Le Château de Fontainebleau*, 1937.

JESTAZ, Bertrand, "Les Italiens à Fontainebleau", *Künstlerischer Austausch*, vol. I, papers of the XXVIIIth International Conference on the History of Art held in Berlin in 1992, Berlin 1993, pp. 93–101.

L'École de Fontainebleau, exhibition catalogue, Paris, Grand Palais, 1972 –1973.

LOSSKY, Boris, "La réédification de la galerie de Diane au château de Fontainebleau sous le Premier Empire", *Archives de l'art français*, vol. 24 (1969), pp. 165–199.

PALUSTRE, Léon, *La Renaissance en France*, 1879-1885, vol. I, pp. 73 ff.

PERCIER, Charles, Original drawings, library of the Institut de France, manuscripts 1014, 1015, 1016.

PFNOR, Rodolphe, *Monographie du palais de Fontainebleau, dessinée et gravée par M. Rodolphe Pfnor, accompagnée d'un texte de J.-J. Champollion-Figeac*, 1863–1885.

PRESSOUYRE, Sylvia, "Les fautes de Primatice à Fontainebleau", *Bulletin monumental*, 1969, pp. 223–239.

ROY, Maurice, *Artistes et monuments de la Renaissance en France*, vol. I (1929).

SAMOYAULT, Jean-Pierre, *Guide du musée national du château de Fontainebleau*, 1991.
– "Fontainebleau - château", *Guide du Patrimoine Île-de-France*, 1994, pp. 268–308.
– "Fontainebleau", *Les Gabriel*, exhibition catalogue, Paris 1982, pp. 34– 41 and 214-231.

SERLIO, Sebastiano, Book VI "Habitationi di tutti li gradi degli homini". Manuscript from the Staatsbibliothek, Munich, 1547–1554, published in Milan in 1966 by M. Rosci. Manuscript from the Avery Library, New York, 1541–1547, published in New York in 1978 by M.N. Rosenfeld.

SMITH, Marc H., "La première description de Fontainebleau", *Revue de l'art*, no. 91 (1991), pp. 44–46.
– "Les diplomates italiens observateurs et conseillers artistiques à la cour de François Ier", *Histoire de l'art*, no. 35–36, October 1996, pp. 27– 37.

TOLNAY, Charles de, "L'Hercule de Michel-Ange à Fontainebleau", *Gazette des Beaux-Arts*, 1964, pp. 125–140.

ZERNER, Henri, *École de Fontainebleau, gravure*, 1969.
– *L'Art de la Renaissance en France. L'invention du classicisme*, 1996.

All works are held at the château of Fontainebleau, unless otherwise indicated.
Photographs are by Georges Fessy except for those where © is specified.

Cover: *The horseshoe-shaped flight of steps in the Cour du Cheval Blanc,* detail.

p. 6 – *Espagnolette from a window in the Queen's boudoir,* by Pitoin.

TIME

P. 8–9 – *View of the Cour des Fontaines at Fontainebleau.* Engraving by Israël Silvestre, mid-seventeenth century. Paris, BnF, print-room.

Chapter I: FRANCIS I

P. 10 – Jean Clouet, *Portrait of Francis I (1494–1547),* c. 1535. Oil on wood, 96 × 74 cm. Paris, Louvre. © RMN-Photo Lewandowski.

P. 16–17 – *Galerie François Premier.*

P. 20 – *Mars and Venus.* Drawing by Rosso Fiorentino, 1530. Pen and black ink, brown and white wash, heightened with white, traces of black chalk, 43 × 34 cm. Paris, Louvre, Department of Graphic Art. © RMN-Photo Berizzi.

P. 21 top – *Portrait of Rosso (1494–1540).* Engraving after a drawing by Passerotti, published in *Vite de' più eccellenti Pittori, Scultori e Architetti italiani* by Vasari in 1550. DR.

P. 21 bottom – *Cleobis and Biton.* Tapestry, c. 1539-1544. 332 × 638 cm. Vienna, Kunsthistorisches Museum.

P. 22 – *Portrait of Primaticcio (1504-1570).* Anonymous engraving published in *Vite de' più eccellenti Pittori, Scultori e Architetti italiani* by Vasari in 1568. DR.

P. 23 – *Story of Psyche.* Drawing by Primaticcio after Giulio Romano, c. 1532. Brown wash, pen, heightened with white, 30 × 76.8 cm. Paris, Louvre, Department of Graphic Art. © RMN-Photo Berizzi.

P. 24 – *Chimney-piece in the bedchamber of Queen Eleanor, now Salon François Premier.*

P. 25 top – *Bedchamber of the Duchess of Étampes.* © RMN-Photo Lagiewski.

P. 25 bottom – *Apelles painting Alexander and Campaspe.* Engraving by Léon Davent after Primaticcio, c. 1544. 34.1 × 24 cm. Paris, BnF, print-room.

P. 26 left – Primaticcio, *Commodus Hercules.* Bronze replica after the marble antique, 1541–1543.

P. 26 right – Primaticcio, *Apollo Belvedere.* Bronze replica after the marble antique, 1541–1543.

P. 27 – Primaticcio, *Ariadne of the Vatican.* Bronze replica after the marble antique, 1541–1543.

p. 30 – *Decoration for the Porte Dorée: satyr.* Drawing by Benvenuto Cellini c. 1543. Pen and sepia wash, 41.5 × 20.2 cm. Washington, National Gallery of Art, Woodner Collection. DR.

P. 31 left and right – *Decoration for the Porte Dorée.* After Benvenuto Cellini, *Victories holding a torch.* Plaster, 137 × 139 cm. Paris, Louvre. © RMN.

P. 31 middle – *Decoration for the Porte Dorée.* Benvenuto Cellini, *The nymph of Fontainebleau.* Bronze, 203 × 409 cm. Paris, Louvre. © RMN-Photo Jean.

P. 32 – Benvenuto Cellini, *Salt cellar for Francis I,* 1540–1543. Silver and enamel, ebony base, 26 × 33.5 cm. Vienna, Kunsthistorisches Museum.

Chapter II: FROM HENRI II TO HENRI IV

P. 34 – *Door of the Salle de Bal.*

P. 37 left – Studio of François Clouet, *Portrait of Henri II (1519–1559).* Oil on wood, 35 × 20 cm. Paris, Louvre. © RMN-Photo Lewandowski.

P. 37 right – Studio of François Clouet, *Portrait of Charles IX (1550–1574).* Oil on wood, 31 × 17 cm. Paris, Louvre. © RMN-Photo Blot.

P. 38 – Antoine Caron, *The Massacres perpetrated by the Triumvirate,* 1566. Oil on canvas, 116 × 195 cm. Paris, Louvre. © RMN-Photo Blot and Schermans.

P. 39 – *Water festivity at Fontainebleau,* tapestry from the *Valois tapestries.* Cartoon by Lucas de Heere after a drawing by Antoine Caron, c. 1588. 403 × 339 cm. Florence, Uffizi gallery. © Scala, Florence.

P. 40 – *Base and capital of one of the two Ionic columns designed by Philibert De l'Orme for the organ loft of the upper Saint-Saturnin chapel.*

P. 41 top – *Portrait of Philibert De l'Orme (c. 1510–1570)* published in 1576 in his treatise on architecture. DR.

P. 41 bottom – *The organ loft in the upper Saint-Saturnin chapel.*

P. 42 left – *Ceiling of the bedchamber of Henri II.*

P. 42 right – *Chimney-piece in the bedchamber of Henri II, the front of the canopy.*

P. 43 – *Chimney-piece in the Salle de Bal.* © RMN.

P. 47 – French school, sixteenth century, *Portrait of Henri IV.* Oil on canvas, 115 × 99 cm (arched). Versailles, musée national du Château. © RMN.

P. 48 top middle – *Part of the Belle Cheminée.* Mathieu Jacquet known as Grenoble, *Equestrian statue of Henri IV.* Marble. Paris, Louvre. © RMN-Photo Arnaudet.

P. 48 top right and left – *Part of the Belle Cheminée.* Mathieu Jacquet known as Grenoble, *Clemency and Peace.* Marble.

P. 48 middle right – *Part of the Belle Cheminée.* Mathieu Jacquet known as Grenoble, *Winged Venus.* Marble. Paris, Louvre. © RMN-Photo Beck-Coppola.

P. 48 middle – *Part of the Belle Cheminée.* Mathieu Jacquet known as Grenoble, *The battle of Ivry and the surrender of Mantes.* Marble. Paris, Louvre. © RMN-Photo Beck-Coppola.

P. 48 bottom – *Part of the Belle Cheminée.* Mathieu Jacquet known as Grenoble, *Cherubim bearing a royal crown.* Marble. Paris, Louvre. © RMN.

P. 49 – *The Belle Cheminée,* measured drawing by François d'Orbay, 1676, detail. Paris, Archives nationales, Maps and Plans section.

P. 50–51 – *Galerie des Cerfs.*

P. 53 – Toussaint Dubreuil, *Cybele awakening sleep.* Oil on canvas, 97 × 103 cm. © RMN.

Chapter III THE SCHOOL OF FONTAINEBLEAU

P. 54 – *Salle de Bal,* measured drawing by Charles Percier, 1793. Detail of a spandrel. Paris, library of the Institut. Photo Charmet.

P. 56 top – *The Galerie François Premier in 1840.* Engraving by Alfred Guesdon published in 1837 in *Les Arts au Moyen Âge.*

P. 56 bottom – *Wainscoting in the Galerie François Premier* © RMN.

P. 57 top – Rosso Fiorentino, *Venus, Bacchus and Cupid.* Oil on canvas, 209 × 161.5 cm. Luxembourg, musée national d'Art et d'Histoire.

P. 57 bottom left – *End of the Galerie François Premier,* measured drawing by Rodolphe Pfnor, 1863. DR. Photo Hautefeuille.

P. 57 bottom right – *End of the Galerie François Premier,* measured drawing by François d'Orbay, 1676, detail. Paris, Archives nationales, Maps and Plans section.

P. 58 – Rosso Fiorentino, *Ignorance banished* (first bay of the Galerie François Premier, south side), detail. Fresco. © RMN-Photo Willi.

P. 59 top – Rosso Fiorentino, *The Sacrifice* (first bay of the Galerie François Premier, north side). Fresco and stucco. © RMN-Photo Willi.

P. 59 bottom – Rosso Fiorentino, *Ignorance banished* (first bay of the Galerie François Premier, south side). Fresco and stucco. © RMN-Photo Willi.

P. 60 – Rosso Fiorentino, *The Elephant* (second bay of the Galerie François Premier, north side), detail. Fresco. © RMN-Photo Willi.

P. 61 top – Rosso Fiorentino, *The Elephant* (second bay of the Galerie François Premier, north side). Fresco and stucco. © RMN-Photo Willi.

P. 61 bottom – Rosso Fiorentino, *The Unity of the State* (second bay of the Galerie François Premier, south side). Fresco and stucco. © RMN-Photo Blot and Jean.

P. 62 – Rosso Fiorentino, *The Fire at Catania* (third bay of the Galerie François Premier, north side), detail. Fresco. © RMN-Photo Willi.

P. 63 top – Rosso Fiorentino, *The Fire at Catania* (third bay of the Galerie François Premier, north side). Fresco and stucco. © RMN-Photo Willi.

P. 63 bottom – Rosso Fiorentino, *Cleobis and Biton* (third bay of the Galerie François Premier, south side). Fresco and stucco. © RMN-Photo Willi.

P. 64 top – *Diana* or *The Nymph of Fontainebleau.* Engraving by Pierre Milan and René Boyvin, 1554, after Rosso Fiorentino. Paris, BnF, print-room.

P. 64 bottom – Couderc and Alaux, *The Nymph of Fontainebleau,* nineteenth century, after the engraving by Milan and Boyvin. Fresco and stucco. © RMN-Photo Willi.

P. 65 – Couderc and Alaux, *The Nymph of Fontainebleau,* nineteenth century, after the engraving by Milan and Boyvin, detail. Fresco. © RMN-Photo Willi.

P. 66 – Rosso Fiorentino, *The Shipwreck* (fifth bay of the Galerie François Premier, north side), detail. Fresco. © RMN-Photo Willi.

P. 67 top – Rosso Fiorentino, *The Shipwreck* (fifth bay of the Galerie François Premier, north side). Fresco and stucco. © RMN-Photo Willi.

P. 67 bottom – Rosso Fiorentino, *The Death of Adonis* (fifth bay of the Galerie François Premier, south side). Fresco and stucco. © RMN-Photo Willi.

P. 68 – Rosso Fiorentino, *The Education of Achilles* (sixth bay of the Galerie François Premier, north side), detail. Fresco. © RMN-Photo Willi.

P. 69 top – Rosso Fiorentino, *The Education of Achilles* (sixth bay of the Galerie François Premier, north side). Fresco and stucco. © RMN-Photo Willi.

P. 69 bottom – Rosso Fiorentino, *Perpetual youth* (sixth bay of the Galerie François Premier, south side). Fresco and stucco. © RMN-Photo Willi.

P. 70 – Rosso Fiorentino, *Venus thwarted* (seventh bay of the Galerie François Premier, north side), detail. Fresco. © RMN-Photo Willi.

P. 71 top – Rosso Fiorentino, *Venus thwarted* (seventh bay of the Galerie François Premier, north side). Fresco and stucco. © RMN-Photo Willi.

P. 71 bottom – Rosso Fiorentino, *Fight between the Centaurs and the Lapiths* (seventh bay of the Galerie François Premier, south side). Fresco and stucco. © RMN-Photo Willi.

P. 77 – *Galerie d'Ulysse: decoration of the vaulting.* Engraving published in 1566 in *Grands Grotesques* by Jacques Androuet du Cerceau, 1566. Paris, BnF, print-room.

P. 78 top – *Galerie d'Ulysse: the celestial globe with the chariots of Diana and Apollo.* Preparatory drawing by Primaticcio. Paris, Louvre, Department of Graphic Art. © RMN-Photo Bellot.

P. 78 bottom – *Salle de Bal,* measured drawing by Charles Percier, 1793. Paris, library of the Institut. Photo Charmet.

P. 79 top – *Galerie d'Ulysse: Venus and the Fates with the sign of Taurus.* Drawing by Primaticcio. Paris, Louvre, Department of Graphic Art. © RMN-Photo Blot.

P.79 bottom – *Salle de Bal,* measured drawing by Rodolphe Pfnor, 1863. DR. Photo Hautefeuille.

P. 80 top left – *Salle de Bal. Parnassus,* measured drawing by Charles Percier, 1793. Paris, library of the Institut. Photo Charmet.

P. 80 bottom left – *Salle de Bal. Parnassus,* measured drawing by Charles Percier, 1793. © RMN-Photo Blot.

P. 80–81 – *Salle de Bal,* measured drawing by Charles Percier, 1793. Paris, library of the Institut. Photo Charmet.

P. 83 – *First Galerie de Diane,* measured drawing by Charles Percier, 1793. Paris, library of the Institut. Photo Charmet.

P. 84–85 – *First Galerie de Diane,* measured drawing by Charles Percier, 1793. Paris, library of the Institut. Photo Charmet.

P. 86 top – Ambroise Dubois, *The Meeting of Tancred and Clorinda at the fountain.* Oil on canvas, 171 × 252 cm. © RMN-Photo Schormans.

P. 86 bottom – Ambroise Dubois, *The Fight between Tancred and Clorinda outside Jerusalem.* Oil on canvas, 197 × 375 cm. © RMN-Photo Schormans.

P. 87 top – Ambroise Dubois, *The Abduction of Chariclea by Theagenes.* Oil on canvas, 162 × 200 cm. © RMN-Photo Willi.

P. 87 bottom – Ambroise Dubois, *The Abduction of Chariclea by Trachin.* Oil on canvas, 190 × 258 cm. © RMN-Photo Schormans.

P. 88 – *The marriage ceremony between King Charles II of Spain and Marie-Louise of Orleans,* 31 August 1679. Engraving by Pierre Brissard, seventeenth century. Paris, BnF, print-room.

P. 89 – *Vaulting of the Trinité church.* Martin Fréminet, *The coats-of-arms of France and Navarre, Christ in limbo, God the Father sending the Angel Gabriel.* © RMN-Photo Blot.

P. 90 – *Scheme for the high altar of the Trinité church.* Drawing by Martin Fréminet. Paris, Louvre, Department of Graphic Art. © RMN-Photo Bellot.

P. 91 top – *Plan of the Trinité church,* measured drawing by Rodolphe Pfnor, 1863. DR. Photo Hautefeuille.

P. 91 bottom – *Elevation of the Trinité church,* measured drawing by Rodolphe Pfnor, 1863. DR. Photo Hautefeuille.

P. 93 – *Women bathing.* Engraving by Jean Mignon after Luca Penni, 1547–1550. Paris, BnF, print-room.

Chapter IV: FROM LOUIS XIII TO LOUIS XV FROM NAPOLEON I TO NAPOLEON III

P. 94 – *Door of the vestibule approached from the horseshoe-shaped flight of steps, leaves of door by Jean Gobert.*

P. 96–97 – *King's bedchamber overlooking the Jardin de Diane, now Salle du Trône.*

P. 98 – *King's bedchamber overlooking the Jardin de Diane, now Salle du Trône: the ceiling.*

P. 99 left – *King's bedchamber overlooking the Jardin de Diane, now Salle du Trône: part of the leaf of a door.*

P. 99 right – *King's bedchamber overlooking the Jardin de Diane, now Salle du Trône: one of the piers.*

P. 100 – *Queen's bedchamber overlooking the Jardin de Diane, now the Empress's bedchamber: the ceiling.*

P. 101 top – *Overdoor in the Queen-mothers' bedchamber depicting Anne of Austria.*

P. 101 bottom – *Ceiling in the Queen-mothers' bedchamber decorated by Jean Cotelle.*

P. 102 – *Cardinal Chigi's audience with Louis XIV, 29 July 1664.* Tapestry from the *Histoire du roi* set of tapestries woven from 1665 to 1680 after cartoons by Charles Le Brun. *Basse lisse* with gold thread, 386 × 587 cm. Versailles, musée national du Château. © RMN-photo Schormans.

P. 104–105 – Jean-Baptiste Oudry, *Stag at bay in the Franchard rocks.* Oil on canvas, 367 × 661 cm. © Giraudon.

P. 106 – *Salle du Conseil.* © RMN-Photo Lagiewski.

P. 107 – *Door of the Salle du Conseil.*

P. 108 – *Ceiling of the Salle du Conseil.*

P. 109 – *Door of the Salle du Conseil.*

P. 110 – *Scheme for the Queen's apartment at Fontainebleau.* Water-colour drawing by Pierre-Marie Rousseau, 1786. Paris, Louvre, Department of Graphic Art. © RMN-Photo Blot.

P. 111 – *Queen's Salon des jeux, or Grand Salon de l'Impératrice: detail of a panel.*

P. 112–113 – *Queen's Salon des jeux, or Grand Salon de l'Impératrice.* © RMN.

P. 114–115 – *Queen's boudoir.*

P. 116 top – *Overdoor in the Queen's boudoir: high relief depicting Euterpe and Terpsichore by P.-L. Roland.*

P. 116 bottom left – *Decoration of the Queen's boudoir: detail of the espagnolette.*

P. 116 bottom right – *Decoration of the Queen's boudoir: panel from the wainscoting.*

P. 117 – Thomas Allom, *The Galerie de Diane,* 1839. Water colour, 32 × 41.5 cm. © RMN-Photo Blot.

P. 118 – *The Galerie de Diane.* © RMN-Photo Lagiewski.

P. 119 – François Gérard, *Napoleon I in his coronation robes.* Oil on canvas, 225 × 147 cm. © RMN-Photo Lagiewski.

P. 120 – *Interior view of the Manège.*

P. 122–123 – Jean-Louis Demarne and Alexandre Dunouy, *The Meeting of Emperor Napoleon I and Pope Pius VII in the forest of Fontainebleau, 25 November 1804,* 1808. Oil on canvas, 98 × 130 cm. © RMN.

P. 123 – Antoine Montfort, after Horace Vernet, *Napoleon's farewell to the Imperial Guard in the Cour du Cheval Blanc at the château of Fontainebleau, 20 April 1814.* Oil on canvas, 98 × 130 cm. Versailles, musée national du Château. © RMN-Photo Blot.

P. 124 bottom left – *Cabinet celebrating the marriage of the Duke of Orleans to Princess Helen of Mecklenburg-Schwerin, 30 May 1837.* © RMN-Photo Blot.

P. 124 bottom right – *Civil marriage ceremony in the Salle de Bal.* Painting by Develly. © RMN-Photo Blot.

P. 125 – *Saint-Saturnin chapel: stained glass windows by Marie of Orleans.* © RMN-Photo Lagiewski.

P. 125 bottom left – *Catholic marriage ceremony in the Trinité chapel.* Painting by Develly. © RMN-Photo Blot.

P. 125bd – *Protestant marriage ceremony in the Salle des Colonnes underneath the Salle de Bal.* Painting by Develly. © RMN-Photo Blot.

P. 126 top – *Theatre by Hector Lefuel: the stage.*

P. 126 bottom – *Theatre by Hector Lefuel: the auditorium.*

P. 127 – *Theatre by Hector Lefuel: the balcony.*

P. 128–129 – Jean-Léon Gérôme, *Reception of the Ambassadors of Siam by Napoleon III and Empress Eugénie in the large Henri II Salle de Bal of the château of Fontainebleau, 27 June 1861,* 1864. Oil on canvas, 128 × 261 cm. Versailles, musée national du Château. © RMN.

PLACE

P. 128–129 – *View of the château taken from the south end of the park.*

Chapter V: LA COUR OVALE

P. 132 – *Cour Ovale: the door to the spiral staircase.*

P. 134 top left – *Ground-floor plan,* measured drawing by Jacques Androuet Du Cerceau, 1579. DR.

P. 134–135 bottom – *Bird's eye view taken from the south,* measured drawing by Jacques Androuet Du Cerceau, 1579. DR.

P. 135 top – *First-floor plan,* measured drawing by Jacques Androuet Du Cerceau, 1579. DR.

P. 136 – *General view of the château,* measured drawing by Jacques Androuet Du Cerceau, 1579. DR.

P. 137 – *General view of the château.* Drawing by Alexandre Francine, engraved by Michel Lasne in 1614. Paris, BnF, print-room.

P. 138–139 – *Aerial photograph of the château.* © VU DU CIEL/Alain Perceval ®.

P. 140–141 – *Cour Ovale: the wing between the Pavillon de la Porte Dorée and the Keep.*

P. 141 right – *Capitals in the Cour Ovale,* measured drawing by Rodolphe Pfnor, 1863. DR. Photo Hautefeuille.

P. 142–143 – *Cour Ovale: on the left, the Pavillon de la Porte Dorée; on the right the Keep.*

P. 144 – *Cour Ovale: in the foreground, the Portique de Serlio.*

P. 145 – *Cour Ovale.* Engraving by Jacques Rigaud, 1738. Paris, BnF, print-room.

P. 146 – *Small view painted as a fresco in the Galerie François Premier.* © RMN.

P. 147 – *Pavillon de la Porte Dorée.*

P. 150 – *Lamp base in the first-floor loggia of the Portique de Serlio.*

P. 151 top left – *Portique de Serlio,* measured drawing by Rodolphe Pfnor, 1863. DR. Photo Hautefeuille.

P. 151 top right – *External steps in front of the portico,* reconstruction by Albert Bray, 1946. DR.

P. 151 bottom right – *Exercise in perspective* by Sebastiano Serlio, 1545. DR.

P. 154 – *The christening of Louis XIII.* Engraving by Léonard Gaultier after a drawing by Jean Le Clerc, seventeenth century. Paris, BnF.

P. 155 – *Scheme for a wing with a loggia* by Sebastiano Serlio, published in 1575 in Book VII. DR.

P. 156–157 – *View taken from the Cour des Offices.*

P. 158 – *The Porte du Baptistère, exterior view, detail.*

P. 159 – *The Porte du Baptistère, exterior view.*

P. 160 left – *Capitals of the Porte du Baptistère,* measured drawing by Rodolphe Pfnor, 1863. DR. Photo Hautefeuille.

P. 160 right – *The Porte du Baptistère, interior view from inside the Cour Ovale.*

P. 161 – *Vaulting over the Porte du Baptistère.*

P. 162 – *Saint-Saturnin chapel.*

P. 163 left – *Saint-Saturnin chapel, cross-section*, measured drawing by Rodolphe Pfnor, 1863. DR. Photo Hautefeuille.

P. 163 right – *Saint-Saturnin chapel, capitals*, measured drawing by Rodolphe Pfnor, 1863. DR. Photo Hautefeuille.

Chapter VI: THE COUR DU CHEVAL BLANC

P. 164 – *Cour du Cheval Blanc: detail of the horseshoe-shaped flight of steps.*

P. 166 top – *Cour du Cheval Blanc.* Engraving by Aveline, second half of the seventeenth century. Paris, BnF, print-room.

P. 166 bottom – *Cour du Cheval Blanc, building forming the back of the court*, measured drawing by Jacques Androuet du Cerceau, 1579. DR. Photo Hautefeuille.

P. 167 top – *Arrival of Louis XIV in the Cour du Cheval Blanc.* Engraving by Israël Silvestre, mid-seventeenth century. Paris, BnF, print-room.

P. 167 bottom – *Cour du Cheval Blanc, buildings forming the back of the court*, measured drawing by Rodolphe Pfnor, 1863. DR. Photo Hautefeuille.

P. 168–169 – *Cour du Cheval Blanc.*

P. 170 – *Cour du Cheval Blanc, buildings forming the back of the court.*

P. 171 – *Cour du Cheval Blanc, buildings forming the back of the court.*

P. 174 top – *Cour du Cheval Blanc.* Engraving by Israël Silvestre, mid-seventeenth century. Paris, BnF, print-room.

P. 174 bottom – *Horseshoe-shaped flight of steps.* Engraving by Israël Silvestre, mid-seventeenth century. Paris, BnF, print-room.

P. 175 – *Horseshoe-shaped flight of steps*, measured drawing by Rodolphe Pfnor, 1863. DR. Photo Hautefeuille.

P. 176–177 – *Horseshoe-shaped flight of steps.*

P. 180 – *Italian-style scheme* by Sebastiano Serlio. Drawing taken from the manuscript of Book VI by Serlio (New York manuscript). Paris, Jacques Doucet Library of Art and Archaeology.

P. 181 top – *French-style scheme* by Sebastiano Serlio. Drawing taken from the manuscript of Book VI by Serlio (New York manuscript). Paris, Jacques Doucet Library of Art and Archaeology.

P. 181 bottom – *French-style scheme* by Sebastiano Serlio. Drawing taken from the manuscript of Book VI by Serlio (Munich manuscript). Paris, Jacques Doucet Library of Art and Archaeology.

P. 182–183 – *North wing of the Cour du Cheval Blanc.*

P. 183 right – *North wing of the Cour du Cheval Blanc: the central pavilion.*

P. 184–185 – *North wing of the Cour du Cheval Blanc.*

P. 188–189 – *Cour du Cheval Blanc: Louis XV wing.*

P. 190 – *Cour du Cheval Blanc, the central pavilion of the Louis XV wing.*

P. 193 – *Cour du Cheval Blanc: Louis XV wing and Francis I pavilion.*

Chapter VII: THE COUR DE LA FONTAINE, THE GARDENS, THE OUTLYING BUILDINGS

P. 194 – *Plate decorated with a view of the Jardin de Diane, 1839-1844.* Sèvres porcelain. © RMN-Photo Blot.

P. 196–197 – *Cour de la Fontaine: view of the Louis XV wing, the Gros Pavillon, the Queen-mothers' wing, the Galerie François Premier wing and the wing of the Belle Cheminée.*

P. 198 top – *Cour de la Fontaine*, measured drawing by Jacques Androuet Du Cerceau, 1579. DR. Photo Hautefeuille.

P. 198 bottom – *Cour de la Fontaine*, measured drawing by Jacques Androuet Du Cerceau, 1579. DR. Photo Hautefeuille.

P. 199 – *Cour de la Fontaine.* Engraving by Pérelle, mid-seventeenth century. Paris, BnF, print-room.

P. 200–201 – *Cour de la Fontaine*, measured drawing by François D'Orbay, 1676. Paris, Archives nationales, Maps and Plans section.

P. 202 – *The château, viewed from the Étang.* Engraving by Jacques Rigaud, 1738. Paris, BnF, print-room.

P. 204–205 – *Gros Pavillon.*

P. 205 right – *Queen-mothers' wing.*

P. 206–207 – *Galerie François Premier wing.*

P. 208 – *Wing of the Belle Cheminée.*

P. 209 – *Wing of the Belle Cheminée.*

P. 210 – *Galerie de Diane wing*, measured drawing by Rodolphe Pfnor, 1863. DR. Photo Hautefeuille.

P. 211 – *Galerie de Diane wing.*

P. 212 top left – *Fountain of Diana.*

P. 212 bottom left – *Egyptian door on the Pavillon des Armes.*

P. 212–213 – *Jardin de Diane.*

P. 214–215 – *Jardin de Diane.*

P. 217 left – *Cour des Offices*, measured drawing by Rodolphe Pfnor, 1863. DR. Photo Hautefeuille.

P. 217 right – *Fountain.*

P. 218–219 – *Cour des Offices.*

P. 221 top left and top right - *Scheme for a Pavillon des Bains* by Sebastiano Serlio. Drawing taken from Book VI by Serlio (Munich manuscript). Paris, Jacques Doucet Library of Art and Archaeology.

P. 221 bottom left – *Jardin des Pins.* Engraving by Israël Silvestre, mid-seventeenth century. Paris, BnF, print-room.

P. 221 bottom right – *Grotte des Pins.*

P. 223 – *Jardin Anglais.*

P. 224–225 – *The Étang.*

P. 226 top left – *The Fountain of the Tiber.* Drawing by Thomas Francine, engraved by Marne, seventeenth century. Paris, BnF, print-room.

P. 226 bottom left – *The Grand Jardin.*

P. 226–227 – *The Étang.*

P. 228–229 – *General plan of the château of Fontainebleau and the surrounding area*, measured drawing by François D'Orbay, 1676. 203 × 91cm. Paris, Archives nationales, Maps and Plans section.

P. 231–232 – Pierre-Denis Martin, *General view of the château of Fontainebleau, after 1713.* Oil on canvas, 242 × 292 cm. © RMN.

P. 231 top right – Pierre-Denis Martin, *General view of the château of Fontainebleau*, after 1713, detail of the Kennels.

P. 231 bottom right – Pierre-Denis Martin, *General view of the château of Fontainebleau*, after 1713, detail of the Capitainerie.

P. 232 – *The Waterfalls.*

P. 233 – *Canal overflow.*

P. 235–236 – *The Canal.*

Index

Index of proper names appearing in the text
(Names of people in normal typeface, place names in bold)

Abel de Pujol, Alexandre, 124
Aigues-Mortes, 26
Alaux, Jean, 76, 82
Alciati, Andrea, 73
Algarotti, Francesco. 105
Androuet Du Cerceau, Jacques I, 12, 14, 18, 153, 154, 155, 161, 172, 173, 186, 191, 192, 198, 199, 203, 216, 217
Androuet Du Cerceau, Jacques II, 46, 95
Androuet Du Cerceau, Jean, 95, 178
Anet, château, 44, 148
Anne of Austria, 95, 102, 103, 178, 202
Appartements des Bains, 128, 149, 203
Aretino (Pietro Bacci), 19
Armagnac, Georges d', 187
Avon, 13

Becket, Thomas à, 13
Bedchamber in the Keep, 74, 76, 95, 149, 151, 211
Bedchamber in the Pavillon des Poêles, 95
Bedchamber of Francis I, see Bedchamber of Queen Eleanor
Bedchamber of Henri II, 124
Bedchamber of Louis XIII, 109
Bedchamber of Queen Eleanor, 23, 24, 96, 149
Bedchamber of the Duchess of Étampes, 24, 248
Belle Cheminée, 45, 52, 103, 124, 209
Beneman, 128
Biard, Pierre, 217
Blois, château, 162
Blondel, Mery-Joseph, 124
Boboli gardens, 52
Bois de Boulogne, 12, 148
Bologna, 38
Bonaparte, see Napoleon I
Boucher, François, 129
Boulle, 128
Bourbon, family, 45
Bourbon-l'Archambault, château, 18, 19
Boyvin, René, 72
Bramante (Donato di Angelo), 152, 220
Bray, Albert, 152

Cabinet Ovale, 92, 109
Canal, 222, 232, 233
Capet, family, 121, 145

Capitainerie, 220
Caron, Antoine, 38
Castello Nuovo, 146
Cellini, Benvenuto, 9, 12, 29, 30, 32, 33, 35
Chambiges, Pierre, 29, 182
Chambord, château, 136, 145, 233
Champverne, Florimond de, 18
Charles V, Holy Roman Emperor, 11, 19, 23, 26, 72, 72, 153, 172, 192
Charles V, (king of France), 18
Charles VII, 14
Charles VIII, 55
Charles IX, 35, 36, 38, 45, 76, 95, 172, 202, 209, 211
Charles of Bourbon, 19
Chateaubriand, François-René de, 121
Chigi, Cardinal, 103
Chrétienne, sister of Louis XIII, 154
Clouet, Jean and François, 38
Collin, Remy, 46, 220
Conciergerie, 216, 220
Cotelle, Jean, 102
Cour de la Fontaine, 44, 76, 149, 171, 172, 195, 198, 199, 202, 203, 204, 209, 210
Cour des Mathurins, 44, 103, 186, 220
Cour des Offices, 46, 103, 220
Cour des Princes, 220
Cour du Cheval Blanc, 28, 44, 45, 76, 108, 117, 121, 131, 133, 165, 170, 172, 173, 178, 180, 195, 198, 203, 209, 220, 228
Cour Ovale, 14, 44, 45, 74, 131, 133, 148, 152, 153, 163, 165, 170, 172, 173, 178, 179, 191, 195, 202, 203, 209, 211, 220
Cousin, Jean, 36
Couvent des Mathurins, 74, 131, 165, 172, 173, 179, 182, 186

Dan, Father Pierre, 29, 179
De l'Orme, Philibert, 38, 40, 44, 45, 82, 92, 55, 162, 163, 175, 178, 181, 182, 191, 198, 202, 203, 204, 209, 232
Des Hôtels, Pierre, 18
Diane de Poitiers, 36
Domenico del Barbiere, known as Domenico Fiorentino, 33
D'Orbay, François, 103, 211, 220
Du Bellay, Joachim , 35
Dubois, Ambroise (Ambrosius Bosschaert), 53, 85, 92
Dubreuil, Toussaint, 52, 53

Egyptian door, 173, 216
Eleanor of Aquitaine, 13
Eleanor, wife of Francis I, 23
Élisabeth, sister of Louis XIII, 154
Elisabeth of France, 153
Errard, Charles, 102
Escalier de la Reine, 152
Escalier du Roi, 148, 152
Étampes, Duchess of, 30, 31, 32, 33, 36
Étang, 38, 44, 172, 192, 195, 198, 202, 210, 220, 222
External flight of steps in the Cour Ovale, 151, 209

Fantuzzi, Antonio, 72
Fontaine, Pierre-François, 84
Forest, 13
Fountain of the Tiber, 52, 223
Francine, Alexandre (Alessandro Francini), 46, 52,
Francine, Thomas (Tomaso Francini), 46, 52, 210, 217, 223, 227, 228
Francis I, 9, 11, 12, 13, 14, 15, 18, 19, 22, 23, 27, 28, 31, 32, 33, 35, 36, 40, 45, 46, 72, 73, 74, 75, 76, 82, 103, 131, 133, 136, 145, 146, 148, 149, 152, 153, 155, 161, 165, 172, 173, 175, 179, 180, 186, 187, 192, 202, 210, 211, 216, 220, 222, 232, 233
Francis II, 35, 45, 73, 153, 199
Frankfurt-am-Main, 40
Fréminet, Martin, 53, 92

Gabriel, Ange-Jacques, 110, 178, 187, 195, 233
Gabriel, Jacques V, 187, 220
Gabriel, family, 108, 187
Gaillon, château, 146
Galerie Basse, 103, 198, 199
Galerie de Diane, 46, 85, 117, 124, 216
Galerie des Cerfs, 12, 53, 216, 217
Galerie des Chevreuils, 52, 53
Galerie des Chevreuils wing, 216
Galerie d'Ulysse, 36, 45, 76, 82, 84, 105, 108, 128, 186, 202, 222
Galerie d'Ulysse wing, 108, 148, 161, 186, 187, 199, 222
Galerie François Premier, 15, 44, 72, 73, 74, 74, 76, 84, 93, 124, 149, 153, 162, 175, 186, 203, 216, 222
Galerie François Premier wing, 195, 203, 204, 211, 216

Gaultier, Léonard, 154
Giambologna (Jean de Bologne), 31, 33
Gobert, Jean, 95
Goujon, Jean, 38
Grand Ferrare, mansion, 232
Grand Jardin, 28, 220, 222, 227, 232
Gros Pavillon, 108, 124, 171, 195
Grotte des Pins, 109, 222
Guérin, Gilles, 220
Guilbert, Abbé Pierre, 29, 76, 84, 103, 105, 109, 179, 187, 228
Guise, 36, 45

Hardouin-Mansart, Jules, 103, 195, 220
Henri II, 33, 35, 36, 38, 45, 55, 73, 76, 103, 149, 153, 161, 162, 163, 172, 175, 199, 204, 211
Henri II's study, 103, 199
Henri III, 35, 38, 45, 55, 95
Henri IV, 27, 35, 45, 46, 52, 53, 76, 85, 92, 94, 95, 103, 105, 109, 133, 136, 152, 153, 154, 155, 161, 178, 192, 209, 210, 216, 217, 223, 232
Henry II, king of England, 13
Henry VIII, king of England, 153
Horseshoe-shaped flight of steps, 95, 175, 178, 191, 209, 210
Hôtel des Ambassadeurs, 220
Hurtault, Maximilien-Joseph, 117

Isabeau of Bavaria, 14, 149

Jacob, Georges, 129
Jacob-Desmalter, 129
Jacquet, Matthieu, 52, 103, 104
Jamin, François, 46
Jamin, Gracieux, 46, 220
Jardin Anglais, 117, 222
Jardin de Diane, 95, 149, 171
Jardin de l'Étang, 45
Jardin des Pins, 103, 117, 220, 221
Jardin du Roi, 223

Keller, family, 217
Keep, 133, 148
Kennels, 228
King's Bedchamber (Francis I), 24, 44, 95, 202
King's Bedchamber (Henri II), 44, 198
King's Bedchamber (Louis XIII), 95

La Muette, château, 12
Lasne, Michel, 52
Le Breton, Gilles, 15, 40, 44, 82, 133, 148, 152, 161, 162, 165, 170, 173, 175, 178, 182, 192, 202, 203, 227, 228
Le Brun, Charles, 103
Le Nôtre, André, 223
Lefuel, Hector, 124, 191
Leonardo da Vinci, 19, 22
Lescot, Pierre, 29, 36
Ligorio, Pirro, 220
Logis de la Chaussée, 223, 228
Logis du Chambellan, 223, 227
Logis du Grand Maître, 223
Loire valley, 11, 12, 14, 19, 55
Louis VII, 13
Louis IX (Saint Louis), 13, 14, 145
Louis XIII, 95, 202, 209
Louis XIV, 35, 46, 102, 103 , 195, 202, 210, 211, 233
Louis XV, 52, 103, 109, 216
Louis XV wing, 108
Louis XVI, 110, 216
Louis-Philippe, 76, 124, 175, 216
Louise of Savoy, 15, 19, 74, 165
Louvre, 22, 29, 33, 36, 44, 46, 154
Lyons, 40

Madrid, château, 12, 33, 145, 148, 162
Maintenon, Madame de, 103
Manège (riding-school), 117
Mantua, Duke of, 23
Marcus Aurelius, 28
Marguerite of Navarre, 38, 73
Marie-Antoinette, 110
Mariette, Pierre-Jean, 84, 108
Mary, Queen of Scots, 199
Medici, Catherine de', 102, 178, 191, 199, 204, 211, 216, 217, 232
Medici, Marie de' 85, 102, 202
Métezeau, Louis, 46
Meudon, 45
Michelangelo, 19, 28, 53, 73, 74, 92, 93, 210
Milan, Pierre, 72
Mollet, Claude, 52, 224
Mollet, family, 52
Montmorency, Duke of, 38
Musée national du Château, 117, 124, 128, 129
Musée Napoléon Premier, 129

Napoleon I, 85, 117, 121, 128, 191, 210
Napoleon III, 124, 128

Napoleon, Prince, 129
Nicolò dell'Abate, 33, 38, 45, 72, 82, 105, 106
Noyers, Guillaume, 95
North wing, 186

Palace on the Île de la Cité, 151, 158
Palustre, Léon, 179
Paris, 11, 12, 14, 28, 31, 33, 121, 151, 158
Parmigianino (Francesco Mazzola), 19, 93
Paule, Pierre, 18, 19, 29, 148, 152, 161
Pavia, 11
Pavillon de la Porte Dorée, 133, 146, 148, 149, 152, 162, 204, 227
Pavillon de l'Étang, 210
Pavillon de Pomone, 128, 222
Pavillon des Armes, 171, 172, 173, 175, 178
Pavillon des Bains, 222
Pavillon des Dauphins, 155, 161
Pavillon des Enfants royaux, 151, 153, 154, 155
Pavillon des Orgues, 171, 172, 173, 175, 178
Pavillon des Poêles, 38, 52, 102, 103, 108, 128, 171, 172 173, 178, 192, 195, 198, 199, 203, 209, 216
Pavillon du Vestibule, 171, 175
Pavillon Louis XV, 187
Unnamed Pavilion, 171, 172, 178
Penni, Luca, 33
Percier, Charles, 84, 85
Pérelle, 199
Perino del Vaga, 19
Peruzzi, Baldassare, 28, 30, 216
Philander, Guillaume, 187
Pierre, Jean-Baptiste, 109
Pilon, Germain, 38
Pio, Alberto, comte de Carpi
Pisan, Christine de
Pius VII, 121
Poêles wing, 102
Pontormo (Jacopo Carucci), 93
Porte Dauphine, 155
Porte Dorée, 133, 175
Porte du Baptistère, 155, 191
Portique de Serlio, 151, 152, 153, 158
Poussin, Nicolas, 84
Pratolino gardens, 52
Prieur, Barthélemy, 217
Primaticcio, Francesco, known as Bologna, 9, 19, 22, 23, 27, 29, 33, 36, 38, 44, 45, 52, 53, 55 72, 75,

76, 82, 93, 106, 117, 124, 146, 148, 155, 172, 175, 178, 181, 186, 191, 198, 203, 204, 209, 210, 211, 216, 217, 222, 223, 233

Queen's apartment, 110, 149, 153, 202
Queen's boudoir, 110
Queen's Salon des jeux, 110
Queen's study, 92
Queen-mothers' apartment, 102, 103, 175
Queen-mothers' wing, 171, 178, 195, 202

Rambouillet, château, 110
Raphael (Raffaello Sanzo), 28, 72, 76
Richeôme, Father, 92
Riesener, 129
Robbia, Girolamo della, 33, 148
Rodez, cathedral, 187
Romano, Giulio, 23
Rome, 19, 27, 28, 31, 53, 84, 121, 152
Ronsard, Pierre, 35
Rosso (Giovan Battista di Jacopo), 9, 19, 22, 24, 26, 27, 30, 31, 33, 72, 73, 74, 75, 92, 93, 120, 149, 222
Rousseau, Jean-Jacques, 105
Rousseau, Pierre-Marie, 110
Rubens, Peter Paul, 72
Ruggieri, Ruggiero de, 33, 38, 52

Saint-André, 38
Saint-Germain-en-Laye, château, 12, 18, 29, 52, 53, 182, 186
Saint-Saturnin chapel, 13, 14, 44, 158, 161, 162
Sainte-Chapelle, 158
Salle de Bal, 28, 36, 40, 44, 76, 82, 84, 124, 161, 179
Salle de Bal wing, 82, 148, 161, 173
Salle des Gardes, 102, 124
Salle du Conseil, 109
Salle du Guet, 153, 154, 155
Sauval, 103
Scibec de Carpi, Francesco, 33, 44, 74, 75
Sené, Jean-Baptiste, 129
Serlio, Sebastiano, 9, 28, 29, 30, 36, 40, 44, 153, 154, 161, 163, 179, 180, 181, 182, 186, 187, 210, 211, 216, 222, 228, 232
Sistine Chapel, 73, 92

Staircase of Francis I, 152
Sully, 223

Tasso, 92
Te, Palazzo del, 23
Tempietto, 152
Theatre, Louis XV's, 105
Theatre, Napoleon III's, 124, 191
Tour de l'Horloge, 173
Trianon, 110
Trinité chapel, 171
Trinité church, 44, 92, 173, 175, 216
Troyes, 14
Tuileries, palace, 204
Turkish boudoir, 110

Unnamed Pavilion, 171, 172, 178
Urbino, castle of, 146

Valois, family, 11, 45
Valle, Palazzo della, 28
Van Loo, Carle, 109
Van Thulden, Theodor, 72, 128
Vasari, Giorgio, 22, 28, 38
Vatican, 72, 76
Versailles, 46, 195, 233
Vienna, 33
Vignola, Giacomo Barozzi da, 33
Villers-Cotterêts, château, 18

Wallop-Calendar, Henry, 73
Waterfalls, 232
West wing, 186
Wing of the Belle Cheminée, 45, 52, 195, 203, 204

Color separation: Offset Publicité, Paris
Printed and bound by Graphiche Alma, Milano.

Chronology of Construction

- Middle Ages
- Francis I (1527–1540)
- Francis I (1540–1547)
- Henri II (1547–1559)
- Charles IX (1560–1574)
- Henri IV (1589–1610)
- Louis XIII (1610–1643)
- Louis XIV (1643–1715)
- Louis XV (1715–1774)
- Louis XVI (1774–1793)
- Napoleon I (1799–1814)
- Louis-Philippe (1830–1848)

Cour des Mathurins

Cour du Cheval Blanc

Jardin Anglais

Jar
de
Dia

Cou
de la
Fontai

Plan of the first floor

1 - Jeu de Paume
2 - Galerie de Diane (Ground floor,
    Galerie des Cerfs)
3 - Pavillon des Armes
4 - Pavillon des Orgues
5 - Trinité church

6 to 9 - King's apartment
6 - Salle du Conseil
7 - King's bedchamber in the Keep
   (now the second Salle Saint-Louis)
8 - King's bedchamber overlooking the Jardin
   de Diane (now Salle du Trône)
9 - Cabinet Ovale or de Théagène et
   de Chariclée (now Salon Louis XIII)

10 to 14 - Queen's apartment
10 - Queen's boudoir
11 - Queen Eleanor's bedchamber
    (now Salon François Premier)
12 - Queen's bedchamber
    (now the Chambre de l'Impératrice)
13 - Queen's Salon des jeux
14 - Escalier de la Reine